the AUTOIMMUNE PROTOCOL

BAKING BOOK

75 SWEET & SAVORY
ALLERGEN-FREE

TREATS

THAT ADD JOY TO YOUR
HEALING JOURNEY

WENDI WASHINGTON-HUNT

FOREWORD BY SARAH BALLANTYNE, PH.D.

FAIR WINDS

Inspiring | Educating | Creating | Entertaining

Brimming with creative inspiration, how-to projects, and useful information to enrich your everyday life, Quarto.com is a favorite destination for those pursuing their interests and passions.

© 2023 Quarto Publishing Group USA Inc.
Text © 2023 WWH Media, LLC
Photography © 2023 Quarto Publishing Group USA Inc.

First Published in 2023 by Fair Winds Press, an imprint of The Quarto Group,
100 Cummings Center, Suite 265-D, Beverly, MA 01915, USA.
T (978) 282-9590 F (978) 283-2742 Quarto.com

Fair Winds Press titles are also available at discount for retail, wholesale, promotional, and bulk purchase. For details, contact the Special Sales Manager by email at specialsales@quarto.com or by mail at The Quarto Group, Attn: Special Sales Manager, 100 Cummings Center, Suite 265-D, Beverly, MA 01915, USA.

26 25 24 23 22   1 2 3 4 5

ISBN: 978-0-7603-7777-2

Digital edition published in 2023

eISBN: 978-0-7603-7778-9

Library of Congress Cataloging-in-Publication Data Available

Design: Stacy Wakefield Forte
Photography: Wendi Washington-Hunt

Printed in China

The information in this book is for educational purposes only. It is not intended to replace the advice of a physician or medical practitioner. Please see your health-care provider before beginning any new health program.

DEDICATION

*To Mom, who first taught me how
to bake, to be fearless in the kitchen,
and that I need never fear the rain
since I'm not made of sugar.*

CONTENTS

FOREWORD

A COMMON MISCONCEPTION OF THE autoimmune protocol (AIP) is that baked goods will be a thing of the past. Not so! There is absolutely a place for AIP baked goods and treats within this healing, nutrient-focused template. The challenge is that the chemistry of AIP baking is very tricky! The ingredients compatible with the AIP diet tend to be low in their binding and leavening abilities—which make them less than ideal for baking. I have certainly experienced more than my fair share of AIP kitchen fails while trying to adapt a favorite recipe.

However, delicious AIP baked goods are in your future again! Wendi Washington-Hunt has cracked the code of AIP baking, so we don't have to. With its exquisite collection of delicious recipes, *The Autoimmune Protocol Baking Book* is the first of its kind, an entire cookbook dedicated to solving our AIP baking woes. She helps us navigate the complexities of AIP baking with gentle humor, warm encouragement, and perfected recipes that use straightforward ingredients and simple techniques.

It should be noted that, to reduce autoimmune symptoms and move forward on the path to healing, baked goods are best consumed in moderation. Too many baked items can crowd out the foods that otherwise offer vital nutrients to the overall diet. To be more precise, the scientific evidence supports limiting added sugars (even natural ones like honey and maple syrup) to 10 percent of total calories.

We can absolutely enjoy a special treat, or a slice of birthday cake, and maintain our focus on nutrient density. And AIP-compliant recipes mean that we don't need to risk an autoimmune reaction to "treat" ourselves. Even better, with *The Autoimmune Protocol Baking Book* in hand, you are spoiled for choice whether you're looking for sweet or savory! Pies and tarts, cookies and bars, cakes, muffins, biscuits and scones, crisps, crumbles and cobblers, quick breads and crackers—this book has *all* of your AIP baking needs covered.

The Autoimmune Protocol Baking Book will guide you through the technical aspects of AIP baking with best practices, how tos, and FAQs. It will provide an opportunity to enjoy baking again, both the process and the delectable results. Happy baking!

—Sarah Ballantyne, PhD
(aka The Paleo Mom)
New York Times best-selling author of
The Paleo Approach and *Paleo Principles*

INTRODUCTION

✚ IN 2015, I HAD ONE of those hard right turns in life that no one asks for. I was living my life quite happily, thank you very much. My kids were getting old enough for me to relaunch the opera career I'd left to raise them. I was ready in every respect to reclaim the dreams I had laid aside.

To get in top singing form, I made frequent trips to New York City for lessons and coaching with some of the best teachers in the industry. I got in excellent physical shape—running, doing martial arts, and lifting weights—to handle the rigors of an opera career. Yes, it was all going according to plan.

Then, everything went south. There was a flood of stressors all at once, including personal family matters, a move from a bucolic setting to a noisy urban one, and a job change. I tried to take it all in stride, but my body was showing signs that something was amiss.

For all my striving and exercising, I was gaining weight. When I sang, I would cough in the middle of a note. I sang flat. My vibrato went wobbly. I felt tired and always cold, almost like the flu was coming on, but every day. Anxiety became a constant companion. Doctors were unsympathetic, suggesting it might all be in my head because my labs were "subclinical."

After some insistence on my part, I was tested by an endocrinologist. I was diagnosed with Hashimoto's thyroiditis, an autoimmune disease where the body's own immune system attacks the thyroid gland. Hmm. The thyroid snuggles up to the voice box. Could this have affected my singing . . . ?

Still, I was told repeatedly that there was nothing I could do for autoimmune disease except take a pill and accept my fate. I begged to differ. During my search for solutions, I had a serendipitous encounter with a bookstore sales associate who had Hashimoto's too. She showed me a section of books about using diet and lifestyle changes to calm autoimmunity. Clearly, there *was* something I could do beyond just taking a pill!

It wasn't really love, at first. I began simply by eliminating gluten. As an avid cook and baker, I found most of the gluten substitutes to be bland and boring. I persevered, though, eliminating dairy and soy, and trying some autoimmune protocol (AIP) recipes. I thought to myself, *What have I got to lose? If this all fails, the only thing that will happen is that I've eaten a bunch of vegetables.*

Soon, I was trying more recipes from blogs and books. Then, I started creating my own recipes. I embraced this new way of eating, dragging my unsuspecting and unwilling family with me. (We've had a few conflicts, including The Great Sweet Potato Mutiny of 2017.) Inventing new recipes, and learning food photography filled the void left by not singing. I have a new creative outlet and a new career path. That hard right turn was not a dead end after all.

With years of AIP cooking experience, there was still one thing I wanted to tackle: baking. I have loved baking since the age of eight when my mother first taught me to bake cookies. By the time I reached adulthood, I was baking everything from baguettes to bagels. So, as a prolific baker pre-diagnosis, I was crushed at the thought of giving up baking because, HELLO: *Baking can't be done without gluten, eggs, and processed sugar, right?*

An idea hatched in my brain—a new dream, if you will. I would write an AIP baking cookbook. I floated the idea past a few blogger friends, who were polite, but basically told me I was crazy. Maybe I am, but the book you hold in your hands suggests otherwise!

For me, baking has always been a way to celebrate people, holidays, first days of school, birthdays, and "just because" days.

It's been my way of communicating welcome, belonging, and care for the people around me. Creating an environment where the fragrance of something baking in the oven permeates the house has been essential to me! Baking means home.

Sure, AIP baking can be challenging, but I believe it can fit into a healing lifestyle, if done with care, and in moderation. After all, *lifestyle* is different than a *diet*. We are embarking on a journey of holistic change, of which diet is only a part. For us to make long-lasting changes, the *style of our life* should be sustainable, and that means an occasional treat. That's real life! In this new way of living, we can leave room for a smidge of something fun. Baking for special occasions can help us feel part of celebrations. We can reclaim the joy of baking we once knew. Most important, an occasional baked item can make us feel normal, helping us stay on our healing path.

I'm honored that you have chosen to take me with you on your journey to wellness, and thrilled that these recipes can embellish your new lifestyle. I celebrate with you, and raise a warm, fresh-out-of-the-oven bagel to you, fellow AIPer. Cheers!

Wishing you great love and deep healing,

Wendi Washington-Hunt

CHAPTER 1

real talk on
AUTOIMMUNE PROTOCOL BAKING

WHAT IS THE AUTOIMMUNE PROTOCOL (AIP)?

If you are new to the world of AIP, welcome! You join a host of people seeking to improve their health using diet and lifestyle changes. Before I attempt to explain those changes, I feel it necessary to say that *I have zero medical training*. I'm just the chick slinging recipes, and there are people much more knowledgeable than I am to weigh in on the subject. Nevertheless, I'll try.

AIP is sometimes called autoimmune paleo, as it is a subset of the paleo diet. However, the protocol reaches beyond diet to include other aspects of healing. The AIP diet begins with an elimination phase: You avoid potentially inflammatory foods for a period of time to allow the body to heal and repair. As you eliminate some foods, others, such as vegetables and fruits, are added in great quantities to flood the body with nutrients. We're talking TONS of veggies; more than you ever thought you could eat!

During the reintroduction phase, eliminated foods are added back slowly, one at a time, so you can discover your unique food triggers. This reintroduction phase helps you determine which foods must be avoided. In the final maintenance phase, you consume the widest and most varied diet possible while avoiding your trigger foods.

Also, be aware that there are a few different versions of the AIP. You may have heard of The Wahls Protocol® by Dr. Terry Wahls, Hashimoto's Protocol by Izabella Wentz, and The Myers Way® by Dr. Amy Myers. For clarity, the template I refer to in this book is the autoimmune protocol as laid out by Dr. Sarah Ballantyne in her book *The Paleo Approach* and subsequent writings. She has modified the protocol in small ways over the years, mostly regarding the reintroduction phases.

Though these AIP versions vary slightly, they share a focus on gut health, avoiding inflammatory foods, and replenishing the body with nutrients through whole, unprocessed foods. Here is a basic, though not exhaustive, list of foods to avoid. For a more detailed list, please refer to Dr. Ballantyne's work.

FOODS TO AVOID

» Beans and legumes of every kind: adzuki beans, black beans, black-eyed peas, butter beans, cannellini beans, chickpeas (garbanzo beans), fava beans, Great Northern beans, green beans, Italian beans, kidney beans, lentils, lima beans, navy beans, peanuts, peas, pinto beans, split peas, soybeans, soy products, sugar snap peas

» Dairy: butter, buttermilk, butter oil, cheese, cottage cheese, cream, cream cheese, frozen yogurt, ghee, ice cream, sour cream, whey, whey protein, whipping cream, yogurt

» Eggs: chicken, duck, goose, quail, etc.

» Grains of every kind, pseudo-grains, and grain-like foods: amaranth, barley, buckwheat, chia, corn, einkorn, millet, oats, quinoa, rice, sorghum, spelt, teff, wheat

» Gluten: In addition to grains, you'll need to be on the lookout for many other sources of gluten, including hidden sources such as beer, some canned soups, and soy sauce.

» Nightshades: ashwagandha, bell pepper, cayenne pepper, eggplant, goji berries, hot peppers of all kinds, jalapeños, potatoes (*except* sweet potatoes), tomatillos, tomatoes, and any spice derived from these foods

» Nuts and seeds: almonds, Brazil nuts, cashews, chestnuts, chia, flax, hazelnut, hemp, macadamia nut, pecan, pine nut, pistachio, poppy, pumpkin (pepitas), sesame, sunflower, walnut, and any nut/seed butter or flour derived from any nut or seed

» Spices derived from nightshades and seeds: aniseed, black caraway, black pepper, cardamom, cayenne pepper, celery seed, chili powder, coriander, cumin, dill, fennel, fenugreek, mustard,

Lavender Thyme Rounds, page 164

nutmeg, paprika, red pepper flakes, star anise, sumac

» Other avoidances: alcohol, artificial flavors and colors, chocolate, coffee, cocoa, corn, emulsifiers (such as carrageenan, gums, and lecithin), processed sugars, processed vegetable oils, sugar substitutes (including stevia and xylitol)

» Any food allergy known to you

FOODS TO ENJOY

» Vegetables: I put this list first because it is arguably the most important food for us to eat. Include as many vegetables (*except* nightshades) as you possibly can! Variety is your friend. Try artichoke, arugula, asparagus, beet greens, beets, bok choy, broccoli, broccolini, Brussels sprouts, cabbage, carrots, cauliflower, celeriac (celery root), celery, collard greens, cucumber, dandelion greens, endive, fennel, garlic, garlic scapes, jicama, kale, kohlrabi, lettuces, mustard greens, okra, onion, parsnip, pumpkin, radicchio, radish, rhubarb, rutabaga, sea vegetables, seaweed, shallot, spinach, squashes, sweet potato (not a nightshade), Swiss chard, taro, turnip greens, turnip, watercress, yuca, zucchini

» Fats: avocado oil, coconut oil, duck fat, lard, olive oil, palm oil, palm shortening, tallow

» Ferments: coconut milk kefir, coconut yogurt, kombucha, kvasses, sauerkraut, unpasteurized lactofermented fruits and vegetables, water kefir

» Fish: anchovies, bass, catfish, cod, halibut, mahi mahi, sable fish, salmon, sardine, sole, snapper, swordfish, tilapia, trout, tuna

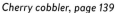
Cherry cobbler, page 139

» Meats: beef, bison, chicken, duck, lamb, mutton, pork, rabbit, turkey, venison

» Mushrooms: button, chanterelle, cremini, enoki, maitake, morel, oyster, porcini, portobello, shiitake (Note: Dr. Ballantyne gives mushrooms their own category because of their importance to the gut microbiome.)

» Shellfish: clams, crab, crawfish, lobster, mussels, oysters, scallops, shrimp

» And also, offal . . . you heard me. Liver and other parts of an animal (e.g., heart, gizzards, kidney, tongue) contain lots of nutrients, so offal is part of the AIP diet. I promise you on the life of my brand-new food processor that I will not be including offal in THIS book!

» Fruit: apple, apricot, banana, blackberries, blueberries, cantaloupe, cherries, clementine, coconut, cranberries, currants, dates, figs, grapes, grapefruit, huckleberries, kiwi, lemon, lime, mandarin orange, mango, nectarine, orange, papaya, peach, pear, pineapple, plantain, plum, pomegranate, raspberries, strawberries, tangerine, watermelon

» Herbs and spices: balm, basil, bay leaves, chamomile, chervil, chives, cilantro, cinnamon, cloves, dill weed (not seeds), ginger, lavender, lemongrass, mace, marjoram, mint, oregano, parsley, rosemary, saffron, sage, savory, tarragon, turmeric, thyme, vanilla bean (not a bean but a flower pod)

In addition to diet considerations, the AIP lifestyle promotes stress reduction, time spent outdoors, social connection, and ample sleep. Autoimmune disease is a whole-body issue, so anything we can do to care for and support the body is helpful.

You can see that the list of foods to avoid in the elimination phase of the AIP is quite long. It can be downright frustrating that the list includes some of the pillar elements of baking: butter, eggs, gluten flours, nuts, nut flours, processed sugar, etc. Which brings me to . . . the challenge of AIP baking.

IS AIP BAKING MISSION IMPOSSIBLE? WELL, ALMOST

I'm guessing that if you love to bake, your heart sank when you read the list of ingredients to avoid. I'm telling you right now that mine did, too, when I first read it. Before being diagnosed with Hashimoto's thyroiditis, I was really into baking, especially breads. Oh, the fragrance of bread baking in the oven . . . it still lingers in my memory.

Take heart. All is not lost! Although baking AIP is not easy, it *is* possible. There ARE ways to bake while on a healing diet. It will require you to use unfamiliar ingredients and techniques that are positively upside-down. For example, the most common substitute in AIP baking for eggs is gelatin. But gelatin behaves in a manner opposite to eggs in the oven. Eggs solidify under heat, whereas gelatin liquifies. I learned this lesson the hard way when I attempted my first pumpkin pie. Needless to say, it was an unmitigated disaster of pumpkin soup that ended up in the trash. I will do my best in this book to keep you from having that kind of experience.

For me, baking has been a joy that I'm not willing to give up, even on a healing diet. If I have to turn my thinking on its head to do it, then, so be it. I would rather do things unconventionally or use unusual ingredients than forswear baking forever. Are you with me? Fantastic! Then, there's a liiiiiiitle something we should talk about . . . .

ABOVE ALL, MANAGE EXPECTATIONS

Those of us who have been around the AIP block a few times understand one very important thing when it comes to baking: **AIP baked goods will never be exactly like what you remember.**

I don't mean to sound harsh, but I have to tell you the truth! You will be able to bake treats that are tasty and satisfying, but an AIP "chocolate" cupcake will not be the same as a regular chocolate cupcake. No matter how much we wish it, gluten-free flours will never taste or act the same as flours containing that gluten molecule. They can never hold, stretch, and spring like gluten flours, bless their hearts.

If the autoimmune protocol were simply gluten-free, we could rely on the proteins in eggs to puff up and hold our morning muffins. Yep, we have to leave out eggs, too. And we'll have to use natural, unprocessed sweeteners in lieu of brown or white sugar, which will affect texture, color, and flavor. We do have options (coconut sugar, honey, pure maple syrup, organic unsulfured black-strap molasses), but we must adjust our tastes a bit.

I think you're beginning to see how an adjustment in your thinking will be necessary to bake in this new way. I'm also betting that you will have disappointments while baking. You might even throw something out! If that happens, try a different recipe. Find one that works for you. Maybe try again later. I will do my best to help you avoid that situation, but again, the truth is, despite your (and my) best efforts, it might happen.

If an attempt lets you down, repeat after me: "I, [name], understand that baking on the AIP is really, really, really hard. I will not give up. I resolve to keep trying until I am victorious—or at least bake something passable." You might want to dog-ear this page. Just joking. Not really.

MIND YOUR MEASUREMENTS

There *are* things you can do to give yourself the best possible chance for AIP baking success. One important practice is to *weigh your flour*. It can be mighty frustrating to have a recipe work one time, then flop when you get a new bag of flour or try a different brand. AIP flours are fussy. They vary in consistency, brand to brand, and even bag to bag.

For AIP baking, there is no one-size-fits-all flour, and no 1:1 substitute for all-purpose flour. Your best bet is to weigh the flour as you measure it, every time. It may feel unnatural at first, but once you do it a few times, you'll quickly get the hang of it, and you'll get consistent results.

If you don't want to weigh your flour, please use the spoon-level-pour method of measuring: spoon the flour into the measuring cup until it overflows, level it off, and pour it in the bowl. It won't be exact, but it'll get you close.

THINK SMALL ON PURPOSE

Most recipes in this book are for items in small portions. The cookie section is larger than the cakes or pies section, for example. This is intentional, for several reasons:

» **In AIP baking, items generally bake more evenly in small amounts.** When I began to develop AIP baking recipes, it was much easier to create a successful recipe if the item was small, like a cookie, for example. Without the structure of gluten and eggs, larger items often didn't cook all the way through, or they were gummy in the middle. I once tried

Graham Crackers, page 163

to make banana bread from a muffin recipe. The muffins were fantastic—but the banana bread? It came out of the oven a gummy brick about 1 inch (2.5 cm) tall. My heart reflected the state of that bread brick—heavy and sunken. That banana bread went straight to the trash. Lesson learned. Think small!

» **It will be better for your healing if you enjoy baked goods in moderation.** It would be irresponsible of me not to address this second reason to think small. If you've been starved for baked goods while on the autoimmune protocol, you might be tempted to go crazy with this book and make all the recipes. Oh, friend. You've worked so hard to reduce your symptoms with this new way of eating. Too many baked goods will crowd out other food items (like vegetables!) that would deliver the nutrients you need to feel better. Enjoy baking, yes, but please remember the reason you are using this diet template in the first place. To keep yourself on a healing path, keep baked goods to a minimum. I define minimum as birthdays, holidays, special occasions, and the occasional horrible, no good, very bad day. Please promise me you will think small on purpose.

» **It is more economical to keep things small.** These specialty ingredients can be costly, especially if you have to get them delivered. Spare your wallet by making smaller amounts of baked goods.

» Keeping baked goods portions small means you can, once again, enjoy some of the things you once loved. They'll also bake better, won't break the bank, and you can stay the course! Good things come in small muffins.

Mushroom Onion Tartlets, page 49

Sugars can mess up your gut microbiome and cause inflammation. It is like that mean girl in middle school who swore on her heart locket that she would never tell anyone what's in your diary but blabbed it to the whole school. Fortunately, we are not in middle school anymore, but sugars are best limited.

I've included several savory recipes, such as biscuits for your special-occasion Sunday brunch. You'll find recipes for snacking while traveling, including several kinds of crackers. I even offer a few appetizers or small-bite items for you to take with you to a social gathering. And I've incorporated vegetables here and there in the savory items to give you a few more nutrients. Hey, we have to get as many as we can!

Savory baked goods can also help with a part of your healing that many people do not notice. As you incorporate more whole foods, more vegetables, and more nutrient-dense foods, while simultaneously limiting sweet things, *your tastes will change.* This is one of the most magical things that happens on the AIP. I used to take my kids to fast-food restaurants regularly, ordering a combination meal with a full-sugar soda. Today, I have no desire to do that. It's not that I've gotten legalistic about this way of eating. It's simply that a meal like that is not appealing anymore. I'd truly rather have vegetables.

IT DOESN'T ALL HAVE TO BE SWEET

Want to "have your cake and eat it, too" where AIP baking is concerned? Here's a trick: Bake things that are savory. You'll get your baking fix without adding sugar to your diet.

ALTITUDE AND INTUITION

A friend of my blog wrote to tell me about her experience with my piecrust recipe. The dough was dry and crumbly, which is not at all the experience I had with the recipe. Together, we tried to troubleshoot it. Was it the lime in her state's water supply? Was it her brand of flour? We went back and forth to no avail.

A couple of years later, another reader wrote to me about a baking recipe, asking what the adjustments were for high-altitude baking . . . *Insert light bulb emoji here.*

I believe *this* is why the first reader's experience with the piecrust recipe was so different from mine. She lived in a high-altitude state, while I'm over here creating recipes, basically, at sea level.

How about you? Do you live at altitude? Do you adjust your ingredient amounts to compensate? I will not be too much help in this department as these recipes were created at a lower altitude, however, there are guidelines you can use.

AIP baking is necessarily half chemistry and half alchemy, and there are several components to consider—the liquid, the fat, the leavening, the type of sugar, the type of flour, the oven temperature, and the baking time. All these components work together to deliver the desired result. Change one component and the result can be drastically different.

HIGH-ALTITUDE BAKING

To make an already complicated situation even more complicated, the changes you need to make when baking at higher altitudes are based on how high up you actually live. They can differ from the changes someone living just 1,500 feet below you must make. It may take a few tweaks and tries for you to get a recipe to work well for you. I suggest applying a somewhat scientific method and change only one component at a time. See the results that gives. Take notes, and scrawl all over your cookbook. Here are some things to try:

» Increase the oven temperature by 15 to 25 degrees Fahrenheit (8 to 15°C) and decrease the baking time by several minutes.

» Increase the liquid by tablespoonfuls relative to your altitude. The higher you are, the more liquid you should add.

» Decrease the leavening a pinch.

» Decrease the sugar slightly.

As you adapt recipes to your location, adjust the amount of flour only when necessary. Start with the weight of flour given in the recipe. AIP baking usually involves a combination of flours, precariously balanced to get a good result, so try not to mess with it too much. Adjust the things mentioned in the previous list first. If you still don't get a satisfactory result, add a little bit of *each* flour. Keep the ratios the same.

The best tool in your toolbox for baking AIP at altitude is your **intuition**. Lean on your past experience as a baker and enjoy the process. Presumably, you already like to bake, or you wouldn't have picked up this book! Although it is true that AIP cake and muffin batters may not look like traditional batters, you probably can tell if something is off. If your cookie dough is crumbly, and there's no mention of it in the recipe, trust your gut and add some liquid. If your cookies spread too much, increase your oven temperature to "seal" the dough on the bottom, and decrease the baking time. Trust yourself. You know more than you think you do.

REINTRODUCTIONS AHEAD

There are a few recipes in this book that contain a reintroduction. I have kept these to a minimum, keeping to reintroductions that appear early in the process. One such ingredient is egg yolk. At the time of this writing, egg yolk is a Stage 1 reintroduction.

As the protocol has evolved over the years, there have been minor changes.

Sometimes, I have felt it necessary to add a reintroduction to achieve a desired result. Banana nut bread would be hard to achieve without nuts, and brownies are so much better with a bit of egg yolk in them. When I use a reintroduction in a recipe, it will be noted with an icon so you can plainly see it. The recipe title will also have the icon next to it. If you are in the elimination phase of AIP, leave those recipes for another day. There are plenty more to try.

AIP BAKING EQUIPMENT

Baking these AIP recipes requires a few pieces of equipment. Presumably, you have an oven. That's a great start. Here are other tools you will find useful:

» **9-inch (23 cm) cake pan**

» **9-inch (23 cm) and, occasionally, an 8-inch (20 cm) pie plate**

» **Baking sheets:** I do not recommend insulated baking sheets. The regular ones yield better results. When baking cookies, we want the dough to seal at the bottom rather than spread.

» **Bread pan:** I prefer glass.

Black Forest Cake, page 104

» **Cookie cutters, pastry wheel, pizza wheel:** To cut out cookies and crackers.

» **Cooling rack:** Typically made from wire, hot baked items placed on them cool much better when air can get under and around them.

» **Digital food scale:** This tool, I believe, is essential for making the recipes in this book turn out successfully. Weighing the ingredients, especially flour, is the only way to be sure that you and I are using the same amount of flour to the gram, no matter what brand or what bag we use.

» **Food processor:** We will use a food processor to purée ingredients, or to make dough. If you do not own a food processor, perhaps you can borrow one from a friend, or invest in one if you are able. A food processor can do things that no other appliance can.

» **Hand mixer, preferably one with a whip attachment:** Lots of mixing can be done using a hand mixer, and the whip attachment is perfect for making frostings light and fluffy.

» **Ice-cream scoop:** This tool is handy for portioning muffins and cupcakes. A 2-inch (5 cm) trigger-release scoop gives you just about the right amount of batter for a standard muffin tin.

WHILE BAKING AIP IS NOT EASY, IT *IS* POSSIBLE. THERE ARE WAYS TO BAKE WHILE ON A HEALING DIET.

» **Liquid measuring cups, preferably heat-safe glass:** Sometimes, you may need to melt shortening or coconut oil in the microwave. A glass measuring cup is handy for this. Liquids are much easier to measure in a glass cup.

- » **Mandoline with adjustable blade:** When you need very thin slices or slices of equal size, use this tool. For baking, it is wonderful for slicing apples and other fruits evenly, so they then cook evenly.

- » **Measuring cups and spoons:** You likely already own these items, but here's a tip: Measuring spoons that are rectangular or oblong fit better into spice containers than round ones. It is also helpful to have several sets of each. That way, you won't have to stop to clean out a measuring implement you used for liquid or shortening to measure dry ingredients.

- » **Microplane:** Sometimes called a rasp, this gadget is used to scrape off the outside peel of citrus fruits, gleaning their lovely oils without the pith. The resulting zest is very fine and easy to incorporate into batters and doughs.

- » **Muffin tin and mini muffin tin:** I use metal muffin tins as opposed to silicone because they are stiff and easier to manage. My recipes use alternate binders, such as gelatin, which make muffins soft when they first come out of the oven, so they need time to set up even before being removed from the tin. You'll use mini muffin tins for bite-size muffins and tartlets.

- » **Offset spatula:** Use this for frosting cakes and cupcakes. It works much better than a straight blade.

- » **One-tablespoon cookie scoop:** I use this in my kitchen so much, and not just for cookies. Using a trigger-release cookie scoop helps you get a consistent amount of dough for cookies, mini muffins, and crust for tartlets.

- » **Parchment paper:** Nonstick parchment paper will be your friend. Many of the recipes in this book require rolling of some kind. It works better to roll dough between two sheets of parchment, rather than flouring your board or rolling pin, which adds flour to the dough and messes with the ratios of flour, fat, and liquid. And parchment can keep your cookies and biscuits from sticking to a baking sheet.

- » **Pastry blender, also called a pastry cutter:** This is the tool I use to "cut in" the fat with the flour for piecrust and biscuits. I've tried a food processor for faster results, but for me, the old-fashioned way works best.

- » **Piping bag with decorating tips:** You don't need this in your kitchen, but it is fun to use to decorate cakes, cupcakes, and cookies.

- » **Plastic ruler:** Does this seems like a weird suggestion? Sometimes, we need to measure the dimensions of rolled-out dough, whether thickness, diameter, or length and width. A plastic ruler can be washed easily. It doesn't have to be fancy! I use one that my kids used in school.

arrow root

cassava

coconut

tapioca

tigernut

» **Rolling pin:** You will need to roll dough for crackers, piecrust, and some cookies.

» **Silicone liners:** Using silicone muffin liners will save you. Yes, they can be a pain to wash, but your muffins and cupcakes won't stick and they're friendly to the environment. Silicone sheet liners are nice to have in the kitchen to take the place of parchment paper on a baking sheet. You'll still need parchment for rolling, but this reusable liner is great to have on hand for lining a baking sheet and it is eco-friendly.

» **Stand mixer:** This appliance has been a standard in kitchens for years. Good to have, again, with a whip attachment.

» **Whisk:** I reach for a whisk several times a day to mix dry ingredients well and incorporate air into gelatin "eggs." I recommend having several sizes.

» **Wooden toothpicks:** To test the doneness of cakes and muffins, insert a wooden toothpick into the center of the cake or muffin. If any batter appears on your toothpick, your cake isn't quite done; if it comes out clean, it is.

» **Zester:** This gadget cuts pieces of citrus zest that are slightly larger than those made by a Microplane, but still avoids the bitter pith.

INGREDIENTS IN AIP BAKING

The first time I saw an AIP baking recipe, I was completely confused by its weird ingredients, so I avoided those recipes because the ingredients were so foreign to me. If you find yourself in the same position, please don't let this hold you back from baking. As we talked about before, baking on the autoimmune protocol requires a change of mind-set—and that includes using unfamiliar ingredients. Fortunately, more of these ingredients are appearing in mainstream grocery stores. Yay for us! I have been able to find most of the flours I use at my regular grocery store and no longer need to order them online. Here's a little explanation of each ingredient to familiarize you with them.

THE FLOURS

Let's start with the most obvious ingredient: flour. Remember, different flours are often used in combination to reach a desired effect. Try to keep the various kinds on hand so you have the freedom to make whatever appetizing recipe calls your name.

» **Arrowroot flour/starch:** I use the words "flour" and "starch" for arrowroot because they both refer to the same thing. Like tapioca flour, it has a consistency similar to cornstarch. It is an amazingly effective thickener for sauces, and it can produce fruit sauces that are like a clear gel. Arrowroot can also be used in baking as a very light flour. It is made from the root of the tropical plant *Maranta arundinacea*.

» **Cassava flour:** This is the granddaddy of all AIP flours, probably the most often used. It is made from the yuca root. Not all brands are the same. Seek a high-quality flour made from a fully peeled yuca root. Cassava flour is neutral tasting and has a consistency most similar to all-purpose flour.

» **Coconut flour:** Use this flour with caution. It is extremely drying and sucks up moisture. Coconut flour is a heavy flour, light yellow in color. There will be times that we need it to soak up some moisture, but I use it only for specific reasons.

» **Miscellaneous flours:** Other flours are acceptable to use on the AIP, such as banana flour and sweet potato flour. They do not get a lot of play in AIP recipes because they are rather expensive and hard to find. The flours I have listed here are those you will find most often in AIP recipes. They are good to have in your pantry as you will use them frequently.

» **Tapioca flour:** This flour comes from the same yuca root as cassava flour, but it is processed differently. Tapioca flour is made from the starchy pulp of the root, ground to a very fine texture, similar to cornstarch. Tapioca flour can give a chewy texture to baked goods and can thicken sauces.

» **Tigernut flour:** Despite the name, tigernuts are *not* nuts; they are tiny tubers, high in fiber. The flour is a bit sweet. It has the consistency of whole-wheat flour. I use this flour in many recipes, sweet and savory. It can lend a slightly nutty taste to something, or with a bit of sweetness, it can taste just like cookie dough.

These flours are very light and tend to fly about the kitchen. If you have a lung condition, consider wearing a face covering while baking.

SWEETENERS

No matter what sweetener you use, your body will perceive it as sugar, so I use sweeteners sparingly. Though we want to avoid regular processed sugar, whether white or brown, there are some natural sugars on the market that are useful to those following the AIP.

» **Coconut sugar:** This sugar comes from the sap of coconut palm trees, not from the coconuts themselves. It is brown with a caramel overtone. The consistency, depending on brand, is similar to granulated sugar.

» **Date sugar and date syrup:** These are sweeteners that I haven't fully explored, but I want to include them here. Both are made from the date fruit. And while we're on the subject of fruit . . .

» **Fruit:** Yes, fruit can be used as a sweetener. It is naturally sweet and requires little to no processing. We might as well reap the benefits of the fruit besides its sweetness.

» **Honey:** If you can find local honey, so much the better!

» **Pure maple syrup:** I'm referring here to the stuff made from the sap of maple trees, not pancake syrup. I had the opportunity to learn how maple syrup is made at a farm in Vermont, and from then on, I've never again complained about the price of real maple syrup. It takes a lot of sap and a days-long process to make syrup. The flavor is lovely.

» **Unsulfured blackstrap molasses:** This particular kind of molasses, a by-product of sugar processing, is dark and rich. It contains less sugar than other sweeteners, and it boasts a few nutrients, too. It is AIP friendly.

ADDITIONAL INGREDIENTS

There are other ingredients you will typically see in AIP baking recipes that are just as important as flour.

» **Apple cider vinegar:** I understand if you raised an eyebrow at this ingredient. Don't worry. You will not taste vinegar in the final product. I typically use this vinegar to activate baking soda, or any time I might need acidity. If you are thinking there might be a bit of chemistry to baking AIP, you are correct. We'll figure it out together.

» **Carob powder:** One of the cruelest avoidances on the autoimmune protocol, in my humble opinion, is chocolate.

Thankfully, we have carob powder, which has the look, consistency, and (almost) taste of cocoa. It is made from the edible seed pods of a fruit. Naturally caffeine-free, it is inherently a bit sweet. I use this instead of chocolate. If you have successfully reintroduced chocolate, please feel free to substitute cocoa powder.

» **Coconut butter:** This ingredient is also known as coconut manna. It is solid at room temperature, and so must be warmed and stirred to be measured properly.

» **Coconut cream:** This is a thicker version of coconut milk. It's not just the fat that rises to the top of a can of coconut cream, unless otherwise indicated. Avoid gums in the product.

» **Coconut milk:** For this book, use a thick, full-fat coconut milk void of any gums, which are not AIP friendly.

» **Coconut oil:** This oil is solid at room temperature. It is made by pressing the meat of coconuts, whether fresh or dried, and so imparts a bit of coconut flavor.

» **Cream of tartar:** Cream of tartar combined with baking soda creates the equivalent of baking powder. We can't use baking powder in AIP recipes because it typically contains cornstarch or rice flour, two things we are trying to avoid. It's just as easy to get the rise of baking powder by combining baking soda and cream of tartar.

» **Extra-virgin olive oil:** This is a surprise ingredient in baking. It works quite well as a fat. The only caveat I offer is that high-quality olive oil can be spicy, which is not the flavor we want in our baked goods. Choose a neutral-tasting olive oil and make sure the oil you choose is not "cut" with other oils, which are not AIP friendly.

» **Food-grade herb and fruit oils:** In AIP baking, we always walk the line between liquid, fat, and flour ratios. It can be helpful to use food-grade oils, such as peppermint or lime, to provide the flavor we need without adding too much liquid. I have a recipe on my blog for blackberry lemon panna cotta. I use lemon oil rather than lemon juice because it would require too much liquid to get the amount of flavor I need in the recipe. These oils are potent so use them sparingly, and do not touch your eyes or nose after working with them.

» **Grass-fed gelatin:** This bovine gelatin is not to be confused with *collagen*. They are two different things. Gelatin is often used as a binder, or an egg substitute. When combined with water or some other liquid vehicle, it liquifies under heat, and congeals when cold. Collagen, on the other hand, will bind

Zucchini Bread, page 151

nothing. It dissolves easily in liquid and can be used in smoothies for gut health, but it is fairly useless in baking.

» **Large-flake nutritional yeast:** These miraculous flakes, made from deactivated yeast, make things taste like cheese.

» **Palm shortening:** This shortening and butter substitute is made from an oil derived from a tropical palm tree. It works beautifully in baking, especially for cookies, and avoids the trans fats of regular shortening. Source a brand that is eco-friendly.

» **Sliced tigernuts:** These are the same tubers that create tigernut flour, but in sliced form. They have the consistency of oatmeal, a texture we can capitalize on in cookies and crumb crusts.

» **Vanilla:** This ingredient causes so much confusion. You may wonder why we can use a bean in baking. Vanilla comes from the pod of the Mexican species of a vanilla orchid. Vanilla powder is typically only available in its pure form through wholesalers, and it is brown. It is also very expensive. That's why it is difficult to find commercially. For our purposes, I use extract. It is acceptable to use extract with alcohol in it for baking because the alcohol, presumably, bakes off. Alcohol-free vanilla extract has a glycerin medium made from rapeseed oil. The amount you ingest in

a recipe is minuscule. Still, for baking, I recommend organic vanilla extract, alcohol included, which will bake off.

BEST PRACTICES FOR SUCCESSFUL AIP BAKING

Baking is an entirely different animal than cooking, requiring more precision, with less room for improvisation. Here are some best practices for AIP baking.

» **Follow the recipe exactly as written the first time you do it.** If you make substitutions (more on that later) or do the method differently because it's what you normally do when you bake, you might end up with less than spectacular results. Remember, we are doing the (almost) impossible thing here, which requires us to think and do differently than we're used to. Once you have some experience with a recipe, feel free to mess with it. But start by following the recipe as written.

» **Use quality ingredients.** Spices and leavening agents lose their pizzazz over time and need to be replaced, especially if you store them over the heat of your stove. Use flours that are fully vetted, not random ones from the market. (I learned this lesson the hard way with a very gritty cassava flour once.)

» **Gather all your ingredients before you mix anything.** This is a lesson my mom taught me when I started to bake, and it goes double for AIP. There is nothing worse than getting halfway through an AIP baking recipe only to discover that you are out of an online-order-only ingredient! Gathering everything you need before you start will help you avoid this problem. My mom also taught me to put away each ingredient as I used it. Doing so not only keeps your space clear, but also gives you a visual cue as to which step you've completed in case you get distracted or are plagued with brain fog. (Ahem. Both hands in the air here.)

» **Measure accurately.** I've heard the motto that "cooking is art, but baking is science." So true! Although cooking on the stovetop is forgiving of us being a little free with the ingredients, baking, especially AIP, is not. There is some serious chemistry involved. See page 16 for more on how to measure baking ingredients accurately.

» **Cream that shortening.** I mean, set your mixer to cream, and get those ingredients good and fluffy. This is especially helpful when baking cookies. Creaming incorporates tiny air bubbles into the ingredients and emulsifies the fats and sugars, producing baked goods with that light, chewy texture we adore.

» **Scrape the bowl.** It may be tempting to hurry through a recipe and not scrape down your mixer bowl, but it is important, especially with a stand mixer. Stuff gets stuck on the bottom and sides, and we need everything mixed together for the recipe to work.

» **Strive to make your items the same size.** This tip isn't just so things look pretty. Having consistently sized cookies, muffins, etc., means they will cook the same, in the same amount of time. I find it helpful to use a trigger-release cookie scoop for cookies and an ice-cream scoop for muffins. It gives baked goods a nice shape, too.

» **Preheat the oven.** Have you ever noticed that most recipes begin with those words? There's a reason for that. It takes a typical oven fifteen or so minutes to come to temperature. That's about the time it takes to prepare a recipe. Make sure that your oven has come to temperature before you put something in it. And while we're on the subject of oven temperature, try not to open your oven while something bakes. Opening the oven reduces the oven temperature and may affect your results.

» **Check your oven temperature for accuracy.** Unless your oven is new, there's a chance it's not performing at the right temperature. The cheapest and easiest way to test this is with an oven thermometer. If you turn the oven dial to 350°F (175°C or gas mark 4) and find that your oven isn't getting there in actual temperature, you can have your oven calibrated by a professional. Your baking recipes will turn out much better as a result.

» **Unless otherwise indicated, bake on the middle rack.** Some bakers suggest turning the product halfway through the baking time so the product bakes evenly. But you have to open the oven to do that . . . I'll leave it to you to decide. You know your oven best.

» **Testing for doneness.** In most baking recipes, the author will indicate to you in various ways how to know when a baked item is done, other than timing. You might see directions to "bake until golden brown," or "until the cake springs back when touched." That will not always work with AIP baking. There are two main reasons for this:

+ Baked items using gelatin as a binder instead of eggs will not appear done until after the gelatin has cooled and solidified. Sometimes, you'll even have to wait before transferring items to a cooling rack because they will be too soft to move. This is not an indication that your baking has failed! The gelatin just needs time to set to come to its full solidified glory.

+ Items baked with AIP flours may not change color as they bake, or even their shape. They may not brown like regular baked items do, unless there are other ingredients doing the browning. An item that goes into the oven an off-white color may still be off-white when fully baked.

With experience, you'll get a feel for when AIP baked items are done. Until then, if your oven is calibrated properly, the bake time for the recipe is all you'll need. Where possible, I give you an idea of what to look for or how to test for doneness. Otherwise, trust the process. We can do this!

USING YOUR SCALE

You will need to "zero out," or tare, your scale, which means you will be measuring the weight of the flour only and not whatever measuring cup or bowl is being used. It's simple to do:

» Turn on the scale. When ready, place an empty bowl or measuring cup on the scale. It won't matter what receptacle you use.

» Push the button that says "zero" or "tare." Now, your scale is ready to ignore the weight of the bowl or whatever receptacle you are using.

Let baked goods cool before you dive in. This tip is specific to AIP baking where, most often, gelatin is used as a binder and it liquifies under heat. This means we must control our urges to go face-first into that muffin, so the gelatin has time to set up while it cools. Often (it depends on the recipe), it is best to let the item cool right in the pan before transferring it to a cooling rack. Give the gelatin a chance to do its job so your baked goods don't fall apart as you remove them from the pan.

Cool before frosting. Be sure that cookies, cakes, and cupcakes are *completely cooled* before smoothing on some frosting if you want to avoid having that frosting melt, droop, and lose its shape before serving.

Use caution when doubling recipes. I don't know why, but whenever I double an AIP baking recipe, it hasn't turned out well. Maybe it's that alchemy factor. Who knows?

But because we're on a healing protocol, it's probably best to keep baked goods to a minimum anyway.

Smooth cake batter with an offset spatula. Traditional cake batter is runny, but in AIP baking, cake batters are often stiff. Using an offset spatula to smooth the batter will give your cake a better look. If you want a smooth top for frosting, you can turn the cake upside-down, or cut off the domed top with a cake cutter made just for this purpose, or a serrated knife.

Substitute at your own risk. Every blogger I know has had a commenter express frustration that a recipe didn't work, usually stating that they followed the recipe exactly—except for X, Y, and Z substitution . . . . If you see a recipe here with an ingredient you are sensitive to, it may be best to try another recipe. You could try a substitution, but understand that it will absolutely change the recipe results.

MORE ON MEASURING

Correct measuring is always important for baking, but probably more so with AIP baking. Those fussy flours! At the same time, we don't need to get so precise as to take all the fun out of baking.

DRY INGREDIENTS

For this book and best results from it, please measure flour by weighing it. Yes, you will need a digital food scale. Yes, it is important and so it bears repeating: It's the only way to be sure that you and I are using the same amount of flour.

Remember to zero out your scale any time you change receptacles. Consider using one bowl to measure all the flours in one baking session, then dumping the measured flour into the mixing bowl. That way, you only have to zero out your scale one time for that ingredient.

If a recipe calls for a tablespoonful of flour or starch, don't worry about weighing it. We have a little wiggle room for that. For all other dry ingredients (e.g., spices, salt, or gelatin), scoop your measuring spoon into the ingredient, level it off, then pour it into the bowl.

FRUITS AND VEGETABLES

When a recipe contains fruit or vegetables, the wording of the measurement is important. For instance, if the recipe says, "1 cup cherries, halved and pitted," measure 1 cup of cherries first, then halve and pit them. If it says, "1 cup halved and pitted cherries," pit and halve the cherries before measuring. Cherries that are halved and pitted take up less room in the measuring cup, so you'd have more cherries in the recipe than if you measured them before cutting them.

LIQUIDS AND SHORTENING

For liquid ingredients, use a liquid measuring cup (i.e., a cup for measuring liquids, not a cup made of liquid!), which is designed just for this purpose. With a clear measuring cup, you can see the measurement line to the top of the liquid. With a regular measuring cup, the opportunity exists to overfill the cup, and then spill it. It's so much easier to use a liquid measuring cup. As you measure, place the measuring cup on a flat surface, and look at it from eye level. You will not get a good read on the amount if you hold the cup up in the air!

For shortening, make sure there are no bubbles in the shortening in the measuring cup. Press the shortening firmly into the sides of the cup, add a little more, and press again. When the cup is full, level it off, then scrape out the shortening with a flexible spatula to ensure that all the shortening makes it into the recipe.

DIVIDED INGREDIENTS

If an ingredient includes the word "divided" that means it will be used more than once in the recipe. The recipe author is telling you the total amount of the ingredient you will need, but that the ingredient will be added in divided portions.

ICING, FROSTING, AND PIPING TIPS

Let's talk about the difference between icing and frosting. Are the terms interchangeable? Not really. Let's define them.

» **Icing** is thinner than frosting and it can be drizzled or spread. If we're getting technical, icing that is thin enough to drizzle is actually a glaze. Think glazed doughnuts. It is made with confectioners' sugar and some liquid, such as milk. That's not going to work for us on the AIP.

I make icing using arrowroot (the consistency of confectioners' sugar), a sweetener, and maybe a flavoring, such as lemon juice or vanilla extract. When icing your baked goods, it is helpful to place the items on a rack, then place the rack on a baking sheet. The icing drips will then fall onto the baking sheet instead of all over your counter.

» **Frosting** is the thick, opaque stuff used to slather cakes and to pipe embellishments. It is made with shortening, cream cheese, or butter and confectioners' sugar. For AIP, I use palm oil shortening, arrowroot, a sweetener, and flavoring.

To do some fancy piping, you might need to add more arrowroot to make the frosting stiffer. Use an offset spatula to apply frosting, being careful of spreading the frosting too thin or you risk getting cake crumbs mixed into your frosting. To make the job easier, consider purchasing a rotating cake stand for decorating. It allows you to spin the cake with one hand and hold a spatula or cake comb in the other for even application.

» **Piping** is the technique of applying frosting through a decorative tip from a piping bag fitted with a coupler. It takes some practice to do it well, so please do not be discouraged if your piping does not look like you want it to at first. Piping bags are cone-shaped and can be disposable or re-usable. For disposable bags, you need to cut off the tip from the end of the bag. Where you cut it will be dependent upon the size of coupler you are using. You can also just nip off the very end of the bag for fine work without a coupler and decorating tip.

Using your coupler as a guide, cut a disposable bag with a pair of scissors so the coupler will just go through the opening, with the threading showing. (Washable, re-usable bags are already cut.) Remove the ring from the coupler. Point the coupler down into the bag and work it through so the threading on it shows. Place your decorating tip on the coupler. Place the ring over the tip onto the coupler and screw it on, right on top of the bag. Make sure no frosting can leak out. To help you fill the bag, place it tip-side down in a drinking glass, and fold the bag over the edges of the glass. Now, you can spoon the frosting into the bag.

Twist the end of the bag right at the edge of the frosting, avoiding any air bubbles. Using your dominant hand (this is the hand that will do the squeezing), grip the twisted part of the bag in the web between your thumb and index finger. Use your other hand as a guide. Before you apply any frosting to your cake, squeeze some frosting out onto a plate to ensure there are no bubbles in it. (You don't want a blow out on your cake!)

You can take a few practice runs on the plate and reuse the frosting if you like. With the bag pointed at a 45-degree angle toward your subject, squeeze and move the frosting along the cake, thinking, "Squeeze and release. Squeeze and release." Soon, you'll get a rhythm going and your embellishments will all be the same size. Practice, practice, practice . . .

HOLIDAYS AND SPECIAL OCCASIONS

Let's get one thing straight. You decide what a special occasion is! If it is your dog's birthday, or the first day of spring, you get to celebrate it. Personally, I think the more celebrating we can do of life, the happier we will be. Celebrate that you are here today!

But let's say you are celebrating with friends and family. You put this lovely cake on the table, you serve it, your friends take a bite and . . . it's not what they expect. After years of cooking, baking, and serving AIP dishes, I have learned to inform people ahead that the thing they are about to consume is void of just about everything they are used to. This is especially important for baked goods. We all have emotions tied to baked goods, which can be dashed when expecting something traditional. Be kind. Tell them what they are eating.

Another important reason to explain what's in your baked goods is that some people may assume that because the goods are egg-free that they are also vegetarian or vegan. Most AIP baked items rely on gelatin to hold them together, which is not suitable for vegetarians or vegans.

It is a good habit to tell people exactly what they are eating. I've learned over the years as a blogger that people are sensitive to many and varied things. Even ingredients that are AIP friendly—coconut products, for example—can be problematic for some people. You might save someone a lot of discomfort by informing them of the ingredients you have used.

If you are baking for a special occasion or holiday, consider doing a trial run of whatever recipe you want to present. AIP baking is tricky, at best, disappointing, at worst, and you won't want any surprises on a special day.

If you will be attending a celebration where someone else is doing the baking, it can be a kindness to bring something along for you to eat, relieving the host of the stress of finding something for you to eat, and you get to celebrate along with everyone else. Check with the celebration host to make sure this will not interfere with their plans.

Special occasions often have a fair bit of stress attached to them, and you may be inclined to bake ahead. Some recipes work well for this, such as for cookies and crackers. Others, like cakes and tarts, not so much. Generally, it is better to serve your AIP baked items while they are fresh.

FAQS

» **Q.** I've seen recipes that call for a "gelatin egg." What is that?
A. A gelatin egg combines very warm liquid and gelatin, whisked or whipped until frothy. It stands in for eggs in recipes. A gelatin egg responds to heat exactly the opposite of a "real" egg, however. Eggs solidify when heated, but gelatin liquifies. To make a gelatin egg, start by sprinkling some gelatin on liquid and then wait a bit for it to "bloom." Then, the recipe will instruct you to heat it or add hot (not boiling) liquid to dissolve the gelatin. Finally, whisk the mixture until frothy, then immediately add it to the recipe.

» **Q.** What does it mean for gelatin to "bloom?"
A. When you sprinkle gelatin on liquid, the liquid begins to absorb the gelatin. It looks as if it is growing and crinkling, somewhat like a flower blooming.

» **Q.** My recipe had little globs of gummy gelatin in it. What's going on?
A. Let's troubleshoot. I suspect that one of these things happened:

+ The gelatin was not completely dissolved before you whisked it.

ICONS

Keep a lookout for these icons throughout the book:

The recipe is coconut-free, or the coconut is optional.

Note: There are several recipes whose only coconut ingredient is coconut sugar. Many people who are coconut-sensitive find they can tolerate coconut sugar.

The recipe contains a reintroduction. There are only a few of these.

+ The gelatin didn't have enough heat applied to dissolve it, whether the heat was from the stove or hot liquid.

+ The gelatin egg sat for a little while before being added to the recipe. As soon as the gelatin egg starts to cool, it will solidify, leaving you with little gummy chunks in your baked goods. You may notice that the gelatin begins to solidify in the mixer very quickly with muffin recipes. Don't worry about this too much. It should still be okay because you will add sugar and the dry ingredients right away.

» **Q.** My recipe didn't work at all. I'm never baking AIP again as long as I live. What happened?
A. I know I sound like a broken record . . . but did you weigh the flour? It really is important. I might also ask whether you live at a high altitude. See page 19 on altitude baking for hints on how to handle this. Make sure that you haven't made any ingredient substitutions in the recipe. I've tested different combinations of ingredients to get the recipe to work and the recipe represents the best way I have discovered to achieve a successful result. If you have made a substitution, it will change the recipe in some way.

» **Q.** Yeah, so can I substitute . . . ?
A. No. I don't mean to sound like a big meanie, but nine times out of ten, a substitution will not work. Additionally, although I have tested several combinations of ingredients, I may not have tried to substitute the ingredient you are substituting and so I can't answer your particular question.
   There is only one exception I know of for flour substitutions. Often (but not always), tapioca flour and arrowroot flour can be exchanged. Don't count on it, though . . .

A WORD ABOUT METRIC MEASURING

You will find that there are different metric measurements for ½ cup flour, for instance. The reason for this is that the various AIP flours have different densities, making some flours heavier than others, and with metric measurements, we measure weight, not volume. Additionally, there may be slight variances in the amount of the same flour I'm using between recipes. It's not an error; I'm just being (overly?) exact. *Remember to weigh your flour.*

» **Q.** I'm not much of a baker. What do you recommend?
A. Learning to bake, especially AIP, is a process, no matter your experience. I recommend starting with something small, such as the Lemon Tarragon Crackers (page 165) or N'oatmeal Raisin Cookies (page 56). Your chances of success will be greater than if you go after Dutch Apple Pie (page 46), or a double-decker carrot cake (see Carrot Cake Everything, page 100), for example. Once you get comfortable with these ingredients, try something a little more daring, such as Good Morning Mini Muffins (page 113), Zucchini Bread (page 151), or Bagels (page 146).

» **Q.** How should I store my baked goods?
A. On the whole, AIP baked goods are best eaten fresh. Most cookies, cakes, and muffins can be frozen without ill effects. Otherwise, store them in the refrigerator. Refrigerate pies and crumbles as well. Crackers, if not eaten immediately, can be stored in an air-tight container at room temperature.

Note: I do not recommend freezing piecrust dough. It may be tempting to make the crust ahead and freeze it, but I've tried this, and the results were not pretty.

YOU MIGHT JUST BE MAGIC. YES, YOU

Determination is the secret sauce that will make you successful at baking, and at reducing symptoms. You will need determination for baking—and for sticking with a healing, nutrient-dense diet, and for avoiding inflammatory foods. You will need determination to bake in a way that seems foreign to you, with strange ingredients, and flavors that may seem peculiar at first.

And, if you have made it this far into the book without slamming it shut and tossing it over your shoulder, you must have determination! Excellent. We can do this. We can do hard things. Please do not give up on yourself, or on your baking. If you have trouble with something, reach out. I will do my best to help you along the way.

It will feel difficult, sometimes, perhaps when you are in the midst of a flare, to keep trying, but there are rewards on the other side of frustration. The fact that you are even holding an AIP baking book is an example. If you only knew the number of times I threw something away as I was developing these recipes . . . . Please, keep trying.

You are doing something powerful with this diet template, something so many of us were told couldn't be done. You are helping calm your symptoms, not just with medication (although that is definitely indicated for some), but by eating well, getting more sleep, reducing your stress, and increasing your connection to nature and other humans. You are learning your unique body's form of communication, its likes and dislikes. You are caring for yourself, perhaps for the first time. I'd call that magic.

And when you pull a real muffin out of the oven that was made without one single egg, grain, or processed sugar, you will feel like a boss. You are indeed magic, my friend. Yes, YOU.

READY? ONE LAST THING BEFORE WE BEGIN.

I'm here for you! If you get stuck, please reach out to me. I will do my best to help you get the result you want. I will share whatever tricks I've learned, like a friend whose kitchen you stopped by to ask for a few pointers. I think we can figure this out together.

When you see photos of AIP baked goods on social media, it may be tempting to forget what a tricky thing this is. If you have a flop, you are in good company. We've all had them. Be patient—with yourself, with the process, and even with me, your faithful recipe developer. Remember, you are attempting something that, by definition, should be impossible!

Enjoy the *process* of baking, even if your result is less than desirable. For me, and maybe for you, too, all those nostalgic feelings come back just from pulling out the mixer, the baking sheets, and the measuring cups. It feels like home to have the smells of baked goods wafting from the oven, especially if we are baking for a special occasion or holiday. And, when you produce something that is good enough, you have won. Celebrate.

Happy baking!

CHAPTER 2
PIES & TARTS

Have you ever turned down a piece of pie? Did you care if the edges were not perfectly crimped, or if the side fell off? If there's one thing I've learned about pies, it is that we can enjoy them so much better if we relax.

The purpose of baking, in my opinion, is enjoyment—both in the making and the savoring. So, don't sweat it. Flop the edges of a Basic Piecrust (page 40) over the filling in the Cherry Galette (page 41) without any crimping. Destroy the top crust on your Lamb or Beef Mince Pie (page 48) and dig in. Enjoy your pie, no matter its condition!

BASIC PIECRUST

This AIP piecrust is as close as I could come to the piecrust I remember eating while growing up. Crust is tricky, even without being AIP, but this one is quite forgiving. If it breaks, just mush it back together! P.S. Some readers are adamant about replacing the salt with some form of sugar. I leave that decision in your capable hands.

1½ cups (225 g) cassava flour

¾ teaspoon sea salt

1 tablespoon (10 g) grass-fed gelatin

¾ cup (154 g) organic palm shortening, plus more as needed

1½ tablespoons (23 ml) water

1 tablespoon (15 ml) apple cider vinegar

In a large bowl, combine the flour, salt, and gelatin. Cut in the shortening with a pastry blender until it comes together and looks almost like pie dough.

The "cutting in" step is the most important part of the process. Keep cutting until the mixture resembles dough without any liquid. If you don't see this, try cutting in yet more. If you still have a crumbly mess, add more shortening, 1 tablespoon (13 g) at a time, cutting in after each addition, until you get that consistency. Then, and only then, move on to the next step.

Pour in the water and vinegar. Quickly mix the ingredients with a fork until they're fairly evenly incorporated. Form the dough into a ball with your hands.

On a piece of parchment paper, flatten and shape the dough into a disk, with one hand on top and one hand on the side. This will keep large cracks from forming. Lay another piece of parchment on the top of the dough. Roll with a rolling pin: for a bottom crust, roll to 12 inches (30 cm) in diameter; for a top crust, roll to 10 inches (26 cm).

Slowly remove the top piece of parchment. Place the pie plate upside-down onto the prepared crust. Place one hand on top, and one hand underneath the parchment. Quickly (but gently!) invert the whole thing. Carefully place the crust in the pie plate, pressing it in and lifting off the parchment as you go. If the crust has cracked, just press it together.

For a one-crust pie, crimp the edges and prick the bottom all over with a fork so no bubbles form during baking. Fill and bake per your recipe.

For a two-crust pie, prick the bottom crust, fill the pie, and *carefully* place the second crust on top. Fold over the edges and crimp them. You may wish to vent the top by cutting 4 slits near the center with a paring knife. Bake per your recipe.

CHERRY GALETTE

You will not need perfectionist skills to make this rustic, freeform pie. Roll out your dough, plop in the filling, and fold in the edges. Bake. Eat. Smile—and roll your eyes back with deep satisfaction. You did it!

4 cups (1 pound, or 454 g) frozen pitted cherries

⅓ cup (78 ml) honey, plus 1 tablespoon (15 ml)

2 tablespoons (30 ml) fresh lemon juice

2 tablespoons (18 g) arrow-root flour

1 teaspoon balsamic vinegar

1 Basic Piecrust (page 40)

1 tablespoon (15 ml) full-fat coconut milk

In a large saucepan over medium heat, combine the cherries, ⅓ cup (78 ml) of honey, the lemon juice, arrowroot, and vinegar. Cook for about 9 minutes, stirring and mashing 5 or 6 cherries until the liquid has thickened and the mixture becomes pie filling. If your mixture doesn't thicken after 9 minutes, turn up the heat a bit until it does.

Preheat the oven to 350°F (175°C or gas mark 4).

Make the piecrust dough. Place the dough on a piece of parchment paper and flatten and shape the dough into a disk, with one hand on top and one hand on the side, pressing and turning, to prevent deep cracks. Place another piece of parchment on top of the dough. Roll the dough between the parchment until it is 11 inches (28 cm) in diameter. Slide the whole thing onto a pizza pan or large baking sheet. Carefully remove the top layer of parchment.

Spread the fruit filling evenly over the dough, leaving a 2-inch (5 cm) border. Gently fold the edges of the crust up and over the sides of the filling, leaving the middle open. The crust *will* crack. Don't worry; just press it back together.

Bake for 15 minutes.

While the galette bakes, in a small bowl, whisk the coconut milk with the remaining 1 tablespoon (15 ml) of honey to blend.

After 15 minutes, brush the crust edge with the honey mixture. Bake for 20 minutes. Let cool before serving.

APPLE BLOSSOM TARTES TATIN

A *tarte tatin* is a French apple tart baked upside-down. Here's my take. These beauties are sticky, gooey, delicious . . . and a bit complicated. The components are easy enough to make, but putting them together is challenging. Consider it a "stretch" recipe for baking AIP. If you are up for testing your AIP baking skills, go for it!

1 cup (110 g) thinly sliced, skin-on Fuji apples

2 tablespoons (30 ml) water

2 tablespoons (30 ml) fresh lemon juice

2 tablespoons (30 ml) honey, plus more for drizzling (optional)

1 tablespoon (9 g) arrow-root flour

1 teaspoon ground cinnamon, divided

½ teaspoon sea salt, divided

¼ teaspoon ground cloves

½ cup (67 g) cassava flour

¼ cup (29 g) tigernut flour

¼ teaspoon cream of tartar

6 tablespoons (90 ml) water

3 tablespoons (45 ml) extra-virgin olive oil

Preheat the oven to 350°F (175°C or gas mark 4). Line 4 wells of a standard muffin tin with silicone liners.

In a cold saucepan, stir together the apple slices, water, lemon juice, honey, arrowroot, ½ teaspoon of cinnamon, ¼ teaspoon of salt, and the cloves.

In a large bowl, gently whisk both flours, the remaining ½ teaspoon of cinnamon, the remaining ¼ teaspoon of salt, and the cream of tartar to blend. Using a fork, stir in the water and oil, mixing thoroughly to form a wet dough.

Scrape the dough onto a piece of parchment paper. Form a square patty with your hands. Place another piece of parchment on top. Roll out the dough to an 8 × 8-inch (20 × 20 cm) square; use a ruler to push the edges straight and to measure the square. Remove the top piece of parchment. Cut four 2-inch (5 cm)-wide strips. Leave the strips in place.

Here's where it gets messy. Beginning with the strip farthest from your dominant hand, lay one-quarter of the apple slices, overlapping, starting at the bottom, along the edge of the strip, halfway in. The apples will stick out on one side, resembling a comb. Carefully fold the other side of the strip onto the apples. Roll up your "comb" from the bottom.

Ta-da! A blossom! Now place your blossom upside-down in a liner and repeat with the remaining strips.

Place the saucepan with the remaining liquid over medium heat. Cook, whisking, until the liquid gets thick and syrupy. Spoon equally over the blossom dough and sides.

Bake for 25 minutes. When the liners are cool enough to handle, remove and invert them onto dessert plates. If desired, drizzle each tart with honey for a little extra shine. Serve warm.

BLUEBERRY PIE

Few things say "summer" like blueberry pie. The filling is sturdy enough to make an open-face pie, and can be made ahead, if refrigerated. I like to make a little extra piecrust dough to cut out shapes to put on top as decoration; just bake those separately on a baking sheet for 10 minutes.

2   Basic Piecrusts (for a two-crust pie) (page 40)

6   cups (930 g) fresh blueberries

¼   cup (60 ml) honey

Grated zest of 1 lemon

½   teaspoon organic vanilla extract

¼   teaspoon sea salt

¼   teaspoon ground cinnamon

Juice of 1 lemon

¼   cup (32 g) arrowroot flour

2   tablespoons (30 ml) water

Coconut milk for brushing (optional)

Make the piecrust dough. Roll out one piecrust and lay it in a 9-inch (23 cm) pie plate, gently pressing it into place. If making a one-crust pie, crimp the edges, then prick the bottom and sides with a fork. For a two-crust pie, roll out both crusts and prepare the filling. Place the bottom crust in the pie plate but wait to crimp the edges until the pie is filled and topped with the second crust.

Preheat the oven to 350°F (175°C or gas mark 4).

In a large saucepan, combine the blueberries, honey, lemon zest, vanilla, salt, and cinnamon. In a small container with a tight-fitting lid, combine the arrowroot, lemon juice, and water. Cover and shake vigorously to combine. Add this slurry to the saucepan and place it over medium heat. Cook for 5 minutes, or until the filling thickens, mashing the berries gently as they cook, leaving some berries intact. The liquid will go from pink to lavender to a rich blueberry color.

For a one-crust pie, if desired for browning, brush the crust with coconut milk. Fill the crust, then bake for 30 minutes.

For a two-crust pie, fill the crust, then lay the second crust on top of the pie. Press the edges of the crusts together, trim off the excess, and crimp the edges. Cut vents into the top crust.

Bake for 40 minutes.

Let the pie cool completely before serving. Refrigerating the pie for at least 1 hour will further hold the filling together.

DUTCH APPLE PIE

I am partial to crumb-top pies, and if I'm being honest, it's more about the crumble than the filling! A good apple pie filling, though, gives the topping a beautiful foundation. The trick is to use a combination of tart and semisweet apples so the filling is neither dry nor runny. Using a mandoline to get even, thin slices ensures that all the pieces are done at the same time.

1   Basic Piecrust (page 40)

3   cups (330 g) thinly sliced peeled and cored semisweet apples (Fuji, Gala)

2   cups (220 g) thinly sliced peeled and cored Granny Smith apples

2½ tablespoons (27 g) arrowroot flour

2½ tablespoons (37 ml) water

2   tablespoons (30 ml) fresh lemon juice

2   tablespoons (30 ml) honey

1   tablespoon (7 g) ground cinnamon, divided

¾   teaspoon ground cloves

⅛   teaspoon ground mace

¾   teaspoon sea salt, divided

¾   cup (75 g) tigernut flour

½   cup (75 g) cassava flour

½   cup (103 g) organic palm shortening

¼   cup (36 g) coconut sugar

½   cup (48 g) sliced tigernuts

Make the piecrust dough. Roll the dough between 2 pieces of parchment paper to 12 inches (30 cm) in diameter. Press the crust into a 9-inch (23 cm) pie plate, ensuring there are no bubbles. Crimp the edges as desired. Prick the bottom and sides of the crust, avoiding the edges so as not to perforate the edges of the pie.

Preheat the oven to 350°F (175°C or gas mark 4).

Place the apples in a large bowl. Add the arrowroot, water, lemon juice, honey, 2½ teaspoons (7 g) of cinnamon, the cloves, mace, and ½ teaspoon of salt. Toss to combine. Let sit while you prepare the crumble.

In a food processor, combine the tigernut flour, cassava flour, shortening, coconut sugar, remaining ½ teaspoon of cinnamon, and remaining ¼ teaspoon of salt. Pulse until you have a crumbly dough. Add the sliced tigernuts and pulse a few times, just until the tigernuts look like oatmeal.

Scrape the apple mixture evenly into the prepared piecrust. Spread the crumble mixture evenly on the top.

Bake for 40 minutes. Let cool completely before serving to give the filling time to set.

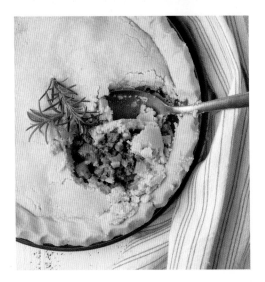

LAMB OR BEEF MINCE PIE

Making a mince pie is a great way to get your baking fix—and make dinner, too! Don't worry about making the crust look too perfect. It's going to be destroyed anyway. In fact, this might be a good way to practice that tricky piecrust . . .

1   pound (454 g) ground lamb or beef

½   cup (80 g) chopped onion

3   large garlic cloves, finely chopped

½   cup (65 g) chopped carrot

½   cup (55 g) diced white sweet potato

¼   cup (25 g) finely chopped celery

1   teaspoon sea salt

1   rosemary sprig, chopped

2   tablespoons (30 ml) red wine vinegar

1   tablespoon (9 g) arrow-root flour

1   Basic Piecrust (page 40)

In a large skillet or chef's pan over medium-high heat, cook the meat with the onion and garlic until browned. Add the carrot, sweet potato, celery, salt, and rosemary. Cook for 3 minutes, stirring frequently.

In a small container with a tight-fitting lid, combine the vinegar and arrowroot. Cover and shake vigorously to blend. Add this slurry to the pan and cook, stirring, until the liquid has thickened. Remove from the heat.

Preheat the oven to 350°F (175°C or gas mark 4).

Make the piecrust dough. Roll the dough between 2 pieces of parchment paper to 11 inches (28 cm) in diameter. Place the meat filling in the pie plate. If you notice extra grease in the filling, leave it out of the pie plate. Fit the crust to the pie plate on top of the filling and crimp the edges. Cut 4 slits in the middle of the pie to vent the steam. Place the pie on a baking sheet.

Bake for 30 minutes. To serve, scoop some crust and filling onto each plate, perhaps next to a big green salad.

MUSHROOM ONION TARTLETS

These tartlets are an AIP appetizer, but you could have them as a meal alongside a big green salad. They are best served fresh as soon as they are made. Note: Alcohol is allowed on the AIP if it is cooked off, which it is here. If you prefer, substitute broth.

- 5 tablespoons (75 ml) extra-virgin olive oil, plus more for greasing
- ¾ cup (100 g) cassava flour
- ½ teaspoon sea salt, plus ⅛ teaspoon
- ¼ teaspoon garlic powder
- 6 tablespoons (90 ml) water
- 2 cups (320 g) finely chopped onion
- 2 drops of honey
- 2 tablespoons (30 ml) white wine or brandy
- 8 ounces (226 g) cremini mushrooms, finely chopped
- ½ teaspoon fresh thyme leaves
- 2 teaspoons (6 g) arrowroot flour

  Finely chopped scallions or fresh thyme leaves for garnish (optional)

Preheat the oven to 350°F (175°C or gas mark 4). Prepare a mini muffin tin by lightly greasing the wells with oil.

In a large bowl, whisk the flour, ½ teaspoon of salt, and garlic powder to blend. Pour in the water and 3 tablespoons (45 ml) of oil. Mix thoroughly with a fork to form a dough.

Scoop the dough, 1 tablespoonful (21 g) at a time. Using a 1-tablespoon cookie scoop will result in consistent amounts. Roll the dough into a ball with your hands. Form the ball into a disk. Press each disk evenly into the bottom and up the sides of each prepared muffin tin well.

Bake for 30 minutes, then let cool. Carefully lift each crust out with a fork and place them on a serving plate.

While the crusts bake, pour the remaining 2 tablespoons (30 ml) of oil into a large saucepan over medium heat. Stir in the onion and honey. Cook for about 20 minutes until the onion caramelizes and turns brown. Do not allow the onion to burn. When onion is browned, pour in the wine and cook for about 2 minutes until the liquid (and alcohol) cooks off.

Add the mushrooms, thyme, and remaining ⅛ teaspoon of salt to the pan. Cook for 2 minutes, stirring frequently. Sprinkle in the arrowroot and stir to bind. Turn off the heat. Fill the prepared crusts evenly with the mushroom mixture; the cookie scoop is helpful here. Garnish, if desired, and serve at room temperature.

RECIPE IMAGE APPEARS ON PAGE 18.

KEY LIME TARTS

The hardest part of this recipe is the crust—and it's easy! Zip it through a food processor, press it into tart pans, bake, fill, and refrigerate. No special decorating skills required. If you've never played with food-grade oils before, I encourage you to try them. They give a deeper flavor than fruit juice, without adding as much liquid.

1 cup (178 g) pitted dates

1 cup (115 g) tigernut flour

1 tablespoon (15 ml) coconut oil

½ teaspoon sea salt

1 can (14 ounces, or 397 g) coconut cream (not milk), stirred

2 tablespoons (30 ml) honey

1 teaspoon alcohol-free vanilla extract

½ teaspoon (2 ml) food-grade lime oil

1 tablespoon (10 g) grass-fed gelatin

Grated lime zest for garnish (optional)

Preheat the oven to 325°F (165°C or gas mark 3).

In a food processor, combine the dates, tigernut flour, coconut oil, and salt. Process until the mixture resembles graham cracker crumbs. Place ⅓ cup (about 60 g) of this mixture in each of five 4-inch (10 cm) oven-safe tart pans, pressing it into the bottom and sides of each, using the bottom of the measuring cup. Place the tart pans on a baking sheet.

Bake for 15 minutes. Let cool on the baking sheet while you prepare the filling.

In a cold saucepan, combine the coconut cream, honey, vanilla, and lime oil. Sprinkle in the gelatin and let sit for 5 minutes to "bloom." Place the saucepan over medium heat. Cook, gently whisking, until all the gelatin has liquified. To get a more accurate pour, carefully pour the liquid into a glass measuring cup, then drizzle it evenly into the crusted tart pans. Refrigerate, uncovered, for 2 hours. Garnish with bits of lime zest (if using) and serve.

PUMPKIN PIE

Pumpkin pie just might be my favorite. It calls to mind many holiday gatherings and all the nostalgia—so I'm pretty picky about it. This version is close to the pie I enjoyed for many years, with one bonus: You only have to bake the crust. The refrigerator does the rest.

1 Basic Piecrust (page 40)

1 can (15 ounces, or 425 g) organic pumpkin purée

¼ cup (60 ml) pure maple syrup

2 tablespoons (30 ml) organic unsulfured black-strap molasses

2 tablespoons (17 g) cassava flour

1 teaspoon ground cinnamon

½ teaspoon ground cloves

¼ teaspoon ground ginger

1 teaspoon alcohol-free vanilla extract

1 can (13.5 ounces, or 383 g) organic heavy coconut cream

1 tablespoon (10 g) grass-fed gelatin

Preheat the oven to 350°F (175°C or gas mark 4).

Make the piecrust dough. Roll the dough between 2 pieces of parchment paper to about 12 inches (30 cm) in diameter and press into a 9-inch (23 cm) pie plate so there are no bubbles. Crimp the edges and prick the bottom and sides with a fork to keep the crust from bubbling up.

Bake for 25 minutes, or until golden. Set aside to cool.

In a large bowl, stir together the pumpkin, syrup, molasses, flour, cinnamon, cloves, ginger, and vanilla.

Place the coconut cream in a cold saucepan. Sprinkle the gelatin over it. Let sit for 5 minutes to "bloom." Place the pan over medium-high heat. Cook, whisking, for about 1 minute until all the gelatin has liquified. Let cool for only 5 minutes, whisking occasionally.

Stir the coconut cream mixture into the pumpkin mixture until well combined. Pour the filling into the prepared pie shell. Refrigerate for at least 1 hour, or until set.

COCONUT CREAM PIE

Coconut is either loved or reviled. If you are a lover of coconut, here's an AIP pie just for you. Now, it won't be super fluffy like the kind with sugar, eggs, and cornstarch. (Remember about managing expectations?) Nevertheless, it works! Toasting the coconut gives it a deeper flavor, and it makes a pretty garnish, too.

- 1 Basic Piecrust (page 40)
- ½ cup (42 g) unsweetened coconut flakes
- 2 cans (13.5 ounces, or 383 g each) heavy coconut cream (not condensed)
- 2 tablespoons (30 ml) honey
- 1 tablespoon (15 ml) alcohol-free vanilla extract
- 1½ teaspoons grass-fed gelatin
- 1 tablespoon (15 ml) fresh lemon juice
- 1 tablespoon (9 g) arrowroot flour

Preheat the oven to 350°F (175°C or gas mark 4).

Make the piecrust dough. Roll the dough between 2 pieces of parchment paper to 12 inches (30 cm) in diameter. Press the crust into a 9-inch (23 cm) pie plate, ensuring there are no bubbles. Crimp the edges and prick the bottom and sides with a fork.

Bake for 25 minutes, or until golden. Let the crust cool before filling.

Place the coconut flakes in a dry saucepan over medium-high heat. Lightly toss them around until they are golden brown and toasted. Remove 2 tablespoons (10 g) to use as a garnish. Add the coconut cream, honey, vanilla, and gelatin to the saucepan. Stir until all the gelatin is liquified.

In a small container with a tight-fitting lid, combine the lemon juice and arrowroot. Cover and shake vigorously to blend. Pour this slurry into the saucepan. Cook, stirring, until the mixture has thickened.

Carefully transfer the hot liquid to a stand mixer fitted with a whisk attachment. Beat for 15 minutes: the first 5 minutes on low speed, the second 5 minutes on medium speed, and the last 5 minutes on medium-high speed. This will cool the liquid as well as aerate it. Pour the liquid into the cooled piecrust. Refrigerate the pie for 2 hours. At the 30-minute mark, sprinkle the reserved toasted coconut flakes on top. Keep leftovers refrigerated.

CHAPTER 3
COOKIES

My journey as a baker began at the age of eight, and many of my baking memories involve making cookies. There was that one time I thought I'd be fancy and crack an egg with one hand over a turning mixer: the egg slipped from my hand, and we had egg shell–studded chocolate chip cookies . . . .

If you are new to AIP baking, cookies can be a good place to familiarize yourself with the ingredients and practices. The N'oatmeal Raisin Cookies on page 56 are an easy first try at AIP cookie baking. Did you successfully reintroduce chocolate? Then, you've *got* to try the Chocolate Chip Cookies on page 60. Here's me, cheering you on to victory!

N'OATMEAL RAISIN COOKIES

If you miss oatmeal raisin cookies, this recipe will definitely satisfy your craving! These cookies are easy to make and a good first shot at AIP baking, if you are new to it. And they're just the right balance between soft and chewy.

½ cup (103 g) organic palm shortening

¼ cup (60 ml) pure maple syrup

1 teaspoon organic vanilla extract

½ cup (60 g) tigernut flour

½ cup (48 g) sliced tigernuts

½ cup (61 g) tapioca flour

1 tablespoon (10 g) grass-fed gelatin

1 teaspoon ground cinnamon

1 teaspoon baking soda

½ teaspoon sea salt

⅓ cup (50 g) raisins

Preheat the oven to 350°F (175°C or gas mark 4).

In a large bowl, cream together the shortening, syrup, and vanilla until fluffy.

In another large bowl, whisk the tigernut flour, sliced tigernuts, tapioca flour, gelatin, cinnamon, baking soda, and salt to combine and break up any clumps that might be in the tigernut flour. Stir the dry ingredients into the shortening mixture. Stir in the raisins.

Using a 1¼-inch (3 cm) cookie scoop, drop the dough onto an ungreased baking sheet.

Bake for 10 minutes. Cool the cookies before removing them from the baking sheet so the gelatin has time to set.

"CHOCOLATE" MINT TRUFFLE COOKIES

If a fudgy, minty truffle and a frosted cookie had a baby, it would be a "chocolate" mint truffle cookie. These cookies are somewhere between a chewy cookie and a truffle. I use real peppermint oil here, not flavoring, so use caution. It's potent stuff!

FOR THE COOKIE:

- ½ cup (67 g) cassava flour
- ¼ cup (24 g) carob powder
- 2 tablespoons (11 g) tigernut flour
- ½ teaspoon sea salt
- ¼ cup (52 g) organic palm shortening, melted
- 3 tablespoons (45 ml) warm water
- 2 tablespoons (30 ml) pure maple syrup
- ⅛ teaspoon pure food-grade peppermint oil

FOR THE FROSTING:

- 2 tablespoons (30 ml) pure maple syrup
- 2 tablespoons (12 g) carob powder
- 1 tablespoon (15 ml) warm water, plus 2 teaspoons (10 ml)
- ¼ cup (52 g) organic palm shortening, melted

Preheat the oven to 350°F (175°C or gas mark 4).

To make the cookies: In a large bowl, gently whisk the cassava flour, carob powder, tigernut flour, and salt to blend. Using a fork, thoroughly mix in the melted shortening, water, syrup, and peppermint oil.

Using a 1¼-inch (3 cm) cookie scoop, portion the dough, roll it into balls, and place the balls on an ungreased baking sheet.

Bake for 15 minutes. Let cool completely before frosting.

To make the frosting: In a small bowl, whisk the syrup, carob powder, and 1 tablespoon (15 ml) of water to blend. Gradually whisk in the melted shortening. While whisking, add the remaining 2 teaspoons (10 ml) of water, *1 teaspoon at a time*. It is important to make the frosting this way, or it will seize, just like chocolate can!

One at a time, dunk the cookies in the frosting and place them on a cooling rack atop a baking sheet to catch the drips. Let the frosting set before serving. I do not recommend refrigerating these cookies because they take on a splotchy appearance from condensation. The frosting will remain somewhat soft, not harden like melted chocolate.

CHOCOLATE CHIP COOKIES

Chocolate chip cookies are a religion with me. I used to make them so often that I had the recipe memorized. I made them for my kids every first and last day of school. They mean home. For me, they must be chewy, only slightly crisp on the outside, and gooey on the inside. This recipe contains one reintroduction, chocolate, because . . . well, you know why.

- ½   cup (103 g) organic palm shortening
- ½   cup (72 g) coconut sugar
- 3   tablespoons (45 ml) water
- 1   tablespoon (10 g) grass-fed gelatin
- 1   cup (118 g) tigernut flour
- ½   cup (58 g) tapioca flour
- ½   teaspoon baking soda
- ¼   teaspoon sea salt
- ¼   teaspoon cream of tartar
- ½   cup (87 g) chocolate chips (Stage 1 reintroduction)
- 1   teaspoon organic vanilla extract

Preheat the oven to 350°F (175°C or gas mark 4). Line a baking sheet with parchment paper.

In a large bowl, cream the shortening until fluffy. Add the coconut sugar and cream again.

Pour the water into a small saucepan. Sprinkle in the gelatin and let sit for 2 minutes to "bloom." Place the saucepan over medium-low heat. Cook, gently whisking, only until the gelatin has liquified. Remove from the heat and whisk vigorously until frothy. Immediately add the gelatin to the shortening mixture and cream again.

In another large bowl, gently whisk the flours, baking soda, salt, and cream of tartar to blend. Stir the dry ingredients into the shortening mixture. Stir in the chocolate chips and vanilla. Using a 1¼-inch (3 cm) cookie scoop, drop the dough onto the prepared baking sheet.

Bake for 9 minutes. Let the cookies cool for 5 minutes on the baking sheet before transferring to a cooling rack to cool fully to set—if you can.

FROSTED PUMPKIN
SPICE COOKIES

These cookies are delicious without the frosting, but if you want to take it up a notch . . . well, I'm not going to stop you! The frosting in this recipe is soft, but if you refrigerate it for a long time, it will become quite hard. Simply bring it to room temperature and it will soften once again.

YIELD : 24 COOKIES
PREP : 30 MINUTES (WITH FROSTING)
BAKE : 10 MINUTES PER BATCH

FOR THE COOKIES:

- ½ cup (103 g) organic palm shortening, plus more for greasing
- 2 tablespoons (30 g) pumpkin purée
- ¼ cup (60 ml) pure maple syrup
- 1 teaspoon apple cider vinegar
- 1 teaspoon organic vanilla extract
- 1 tablespoon (15 ml) water
- 2 tablespoons (30 ml) hot water (not boiling)
- 1 tablespoon (10 g) grass-fed gelatin
- 1 cup (118 g) tigernut flour
- ½ cup (58 g) tapioca flour
- 1½ teaspoons ground cinnamon
- ¾ teaspoon ground cloves
- ½ teaspoon baking soda
- ¼ teaspoon ground ginger
- ¼ teaspoon sea salt
- ¼ teaspoon cream of tartar
- ⅛ teaspoon ground mace

FOR THE FROSTING:

- ½ cup (103 g) organic palm shortening
- ¼ cup (30 g) arrowroot flour
- 2 tablespoons (30 ml) pure maple syrup
- ½ teaspoon apple cider vinegar
- ½ teaspoon alcohol-free vanilla extract
- ¼ teaspoon ground cinnamon, plus more for sprinkling

Preheat the oven to 350°F (175°C or gas mark 4). Lightly grease a baking sheet with shortening.

To make the cookies: In a large bowl, cream the shortening until fluffy. Add the pumpkin, syrup, vinegar, and vanilla and cream again.

Pour 1 tablespoon (15 ml) of water into a small bowl. Sprinkle in the gelatin and whisk gently to combine. Add the hot water and whisk vigorously until frothy. Immediately add the gelatin to the shortening mixture and cream again.

In a medium-size bowl, gently whisk the flours, cinnamon, cloves, baking soda, ginger, salt, cream of tartar, and mace to blend. Add the dry ingredients to the shortening mixture and stir to combine. Using a tablespoon measure, drop the dough by spoonfuls onto the prepared baking sheet (it will take two batches).

Bake for 10 minutes. Let the cookies cool on the baking sheet for 5 minutes before transferring to a cooling rack. Repeat for the second batch.

To make the frosting: While the cookies cool, in a large bowl, cream the shortening until fluffy. Add the flour, syrup, vinegar, vanilla, and cinnamon and cream again. Spread the frosting on the cooled cookies and garnish with a sprinkle of cinnamon.

YIELD : 12 COOKIES
PREP : 18 MINUTES
BAKE : 25 MINUTES

APPLE CINNAMON BREAKFAST COOKIES

Though shaped like cookies, these treats are more like a soft, chewy granola bar. The fruit—yes, zucchini is technically a fruit—is hidden here. Speaking of hiding, if you need to hide the zucchini from yourself or someone in your house, peel it before grating it.

1 cup (225 g) mashed, slightly green banana (about 2 bananas)

¾ cup (88 g) tigernut flour

½ cup (75 g) grated peeled apple

½ cup (60 g) grated zucchini

½ cup (48 g) sliced tigernuts

½ cup (75 g) raisins

⅓ cup (28 g) organic unsweetened shredded coconut

1 tablespoon (15 ml) pure maple syrup

1½ teaspoons ground cinnamon

1 teaspoon sea salt

½ teaspoon baking soda

¼ teaspoon ground cloves

Preheat the oven to 350°F (175°C or gas mark 4). Line a baking sheet with parchment paper.

In a large bowl, stir together the banana, flour, apple, zucchini, sliced tigernuts, raisins, coconut, syrup, cinnamon, salt, baking soda, and cloves.

Using a 2-inch (5 cm) ice-cream scoop, drop the dough onto the prepared baking sheet. Flatten each cookie to about ½ inch (1 cm).

Bake for 25 minutes. Let the cookies cool on the baking sheet before transferring to a cooling rack to cool completely before serving. Keep refrigerated.

"CHOCOLATE" COCONUT MACAROON COOKIES

Confession: I am not a big fan of coconut. But THESE, I like! They are a sort of fudgy cookie, but with shredded coconut. The secret ingredient is coconut butter, a.k.a. coconut manna. Note: It must be softened and stirred before measuring.

- ⅓ cup (75 g) softened and stirred coconut butter
- ¼ cup (60 ml) pure maple syrup
- 3 tablespoons (45 ml) water
- 1 tablespoon (10 g) grass-fed gelatin
- 1 cup (85 g) unsweetened coconut flakes
- ¼ cup (29 g) arrowroot flour
- ¼ cup (24 g) carob powder or cocoa powder (if successfully reintroduced)
- 1 teaspoon organic vanilla extract
- ½ teaspoon sea salt

Preheat the oven to 350°F (175°C or gas mark 4). Line a baking sheet with parchment paper.

In a large bowl, cream the coconut butter until fluffy. Add the syrup and cream again.

Pour the water into a cold saucepan. Sprinkle in the gelatin and let sit for 2 minutes to "bloom." Place the saucepan over medium-low low heat. Cook, gently whisking, just until all the gelatin is liquified. Remove from the heat, tip the saucepan, and whisk vigorously until frothy. Immediately add the gelatin to the coconut butter mixture and cream again. Scrape the mixture back into the saucepan.

Place the saucepan over medium-low heat and add the remaining ingredients all at once. Stir well to combine. Using a 1¼-inch (3 cm) cookie scoop, drop the batter from the saucepan onto the prepared baking sheet.

Bake for 8 to 9 minutes. Let the cookies cool on the baking sheet so the gelatin sets before serving.

CLEANUP TIP

+ Scrape out the saucepan while it is still warm, or you'll have quite a mess on your hands. If the pan scrapings harden too quickly, warm the pan gently on the stovetop and scrape or wipe it out. Wash as usual.

GINGERBREAD COOKIES

I'm so pleased to share this nostalgic recipe with you. I have adapted a recipe for the AIP that came from my great-grandmother! It behaves and tastes just like the one I made growing up. I don't think she would mind that I've adapted it for a healing diet. Enjoy!

- ½ cup (89 g) chopped pitted dates
- ½ cup (125 ml) organic unsulfured blackstrap molasses
- ½ cup (103 g) organic palm shortening
- ½ cup (120 ml) full-fat coconut milk
- 1 tablespoon (15 ml) apple cider vinegar
- 1 cup (150 g) cassava flour, plus more as needed
- 1½ cups (173 g) arrowroot flour
- 1 tablespoon (10 g) grass-fed gelatin
- 1½ teaspoons baking soda
- 1 teaspoon ground ginger
- ½ teaspoon ground cinnamon
- ½ teaspoon ground cloves
- ½ teaspoon cream of tartar

In a food processor, cream together the dates, molasses, and shortening until fluffy and without lumps. You may need to stop to scrape down the sides of the bowl multiple times to get everything fully incorporated.

In a small bowl, combine the coconut milk and vinegar.

In a medium-size bowl, whisk the cassava flour, arrowroot, gelatin, baking soda, ginger, cinnamon, cloves, and cream of tartar to blend.

With the processor on, gradually add the coconut milk mixture through the feeder tube. Add the dry ingredients in batches, processing until the dough comes together in a ball. *Note: If this doesn't happen, your dough is too wet. Add 2 tablespoons (18.75 g) of cassava flour at a time until you have a stiff, workable dough. No worries.*

Wrap the dough in plastic and chill it in the refrigerator for 30 minutes.

Preheat the oven to 375°F (190°C or gas mark 5). Line a baking sheet with parchment paper.

Roll the dough in batches between 2 pieces of parchment paper to no thinner than ¼ inch (6 mm). Cut it into desired shapes and transfer them to the prepared baking sheet.

Bake for 10 minutes. Let cool completely before decorating, if desired.

PIPING FROSTING

+ To make the piping frosting (if using): In a large bowl, using a hand mixer fitted with a whisk attachment, beat ½ cup (103 g) palm shortening, 1 tablespoon (15 ml) pure maple syrup, and 1 tablespoon (9 g) arrowroot flour to blend. Color portions with carob powder, cinnamon, beet juice, blueberry juice, pomegranate juice, or turmeric, as desired, to decorate your cookies.

CINNAMON COCONUT TRUFFLE COOKIES

If you like coconut, this truffle cookie is for you. Imagine a bite of yum that is somewhere between a glazed coconut doughnut hole and a cookie. These should be refrigerated before serving.

½ cup (67 g) cassava flour

¼ cup (21 g) unsweetened shredded coconut, plus more for garnish (optional)

2 tablespoons (11 g) tigernut flour

1 teaspoon ground cinnamon

½ teaspoon sea salt

¼ cup (52 g) organic palm shortening, melted

3 tablespoons (45 ml) warm water

4 tablespoons (60 ml) pure maple syrup, divided

¼ cup (55 g) softened and stirred coconut butter

¼ cup (54 g) coconut oil

2 tablespoons (18 g) arrow-root flour

Preheat the oven to 350°F (175°C or gas mark 4). Line a plate with parchment paper.

In a large bowl, gently whisk the cassava flour, coconut, tigernut flour, cinnamon, and salt to blend. Using a fork, thoroughly mix in the melted shortening, water, and 2 tablespoons (30 ml) of syrup. Using a 1¼-inch (3 cm) cookie scoop, portion the dough, roll it into balls, and place the balls on an ungreased baking sheet.

Bake for 15 minutes. Let cool completely.

In a microwave-safe bowl, combine the coconut butter and coconut oil. Cover with wax paper and microwave for about 30 seconds to melt (keep an eye on it). Alternatively, melt together in a small saucepan over low heat on the stovetop. Whisk in the remaining 2 tablespoons (30 ml) of syrup and the arrowroot. One at a time, dunk the cookies into the glaze and place them on the prepared plate. Sprinkle with shredded coconut to garnish (if using).

Refrigerate for 15 minutes before serving.

CRANBERRY SHORTBREAD TEA CAKES

These cookie-ish tea cakes (cake-ish tea cookies?) are not too sweet, a little soft, and oh-so-right to accompany an afternoon cuppa. Choose dried cranberries with no oils or sugars in them.

½ cup (103 g) organic palm shortening

3 tablespoons (45 ml) honey

2 tablespoons (30 ml) fresh orange juice

1 tablespoon (10 g) grass-fed gelatin

2 tablespoons (30 ml) hot (not boiling) water

¾ cup (101 g) cassava flour

¼ cup (29 g) arrowroot flour

2 tablespoons (16 g) finely chopped dried cranberries (no added oils or sugars), plus more for garnish (optional)

½ teaspoon baking soda

½ teaspoon sea salt

¼ teaspoon cream of tartar

Ground cinnamon for dusting (optional)

Preheat the oven to 350°F (175°C or gas mark 4).

In a large bowl, cream together the shortening and honey until fluffy.

Place the orange juice in a small bowl. Sprinkle in the gelatin and whisk gently to combine. Pour in the hot water and whisk vigorously until frothy. Immediately add the gelatin to the shortening mixture and cream everything together.

In a medium-size bowl, combine the cassava flour, arrowroot, cranberries, baking soda, salt, and cream of tartar. Add the dry ingredients to the shortening mixture. Stir to form a dough.

Using a 1¼-inch (3 cm) cookie scoop, portion the dough, roll it into balls, and place the balls on an ungreased baking sheet.

Bake for 9 minutes. Transfer the cookies to a cooling rack. Garnish with more cranberries (if using) and a dusting of cinnamon (if using) and let cool before serving.

RECIPE IMAGE APPEARS ON PAGE 3.

SNICKERDOODLES

These cookies are puffier than traditional snickerdoodles, with a little more attitude. Can a cookie have attitude? I guess it can if it wants to. I rather enjoy a cookie that bites back.

½ cup (103 g) organic palm shortening, plus more for greasing

4 tablespoons (36 g) coconut sugar, divided

1 tablespoon (15 ml) fresh lemon juice

1 teaspoon organic vanilla extract

3 tablespoons (45 ml) water

1½ tablespoons (15 g) grass-fed gelatin

1 cup (128 g) cassava flour

½ teaspoon baking soda

½ teaspoon sea salt

¼ teaspoon cream of tartar

1½ teaspoons ground cinnamon

Preheat the oven to 350°F (175°C or gas mark 4). Lightly grease a baking sheet with shortening.

In a large bowl, cream the shortening until fluffy. Add 3 tablespoons (27 g) of coconut sugar, the lemon juice, and vanilla and cream again until fluffy.

Pour the water into a cold saucepan. Sprinkle in the gelatin and let sit for 2 minutes to "bloom." Place the saucepan over medium-low heat. Cook, gently whisking, until all the gelatin has liquified. Remove from heat and whisk vigorously until frothy. Add the gelatin immediately to the shortening mixture and cream again.

In a medium-size bowl, combine the flour, baking soda, salt, and cream of tartar. Add the dry ingredients to the shortening mixture. Stir until incorporated.

In a small bowl, stir together the remaining 1 tablespoon (9 g) of coconut sugar and cinnamon.

Using a 1-tablespoon cookie scoop, scoop the dough and roll it into balls with your hands. One at a time, lightly roll the cookie balls in the cinnamon mixture, then place them on the prepared baking sheet (this may take two batches).

Bake for 10 minutes. Repeat for the second batch, if needed.

CUT-OUT SUGAR COOKIES

Holidays are more fun when there are cookies to decorate! These "sugar" cookies are not quite as sweet as the traditional kind, to compensate for frosting or other decorations. Have fun!

½ cup (103 g) organic palm shortening

3 tablespoons (45 ml) honey

2 teaspoons (10 ml) organic vanilla extract

3 tablespoons (45 ml) water

1 tablespoon (10 g) grass-fed gelatin

¾ cup (95 g) cassava flour

¼ cup (31 g) tigernut flour

¼ cup (29 g) tapioca flour

½ teaspoon baking soda

½ teaspoon sea salt

¼ teaspoon cream of tartar

Preheat the oven to 350°F (175°C or gas mark 4).

In a large bowl, cream the shortening until fluffy. Add the honey and vanilla and cream again.

Pour the water into a cold saucepan. Sprinkle in the gelatin and let sit for 2 minutes to "bloom." Place the saucepan over medium-low heat. Cook, gently whisking, just until all the gelatin is liquified. Remove from the heat, tip the saucepan, and whisk vigorously until frothy. Immediately add the gelatin to the shortening mixture and cream again.

In a medium-size bowl, gently whisk the flours, baking soda, salt, and cream of tartar to combine. Stir the dry ingredients into the shortening mixture.

Gather the dough and place it on a piece of parchment paper. Form the dough into a disk, with one hand on top and the other on the side to prevent cracking. Place another piece of parchment on top and roll the dough between the parchment layers until it is ¼ inch (6 mm) thick, but no thinner. Cut out your desired shapes and carefully transfer them to an ungreased baking sheet.

Bake for 7 minutes or less, depending on the size of the shape. Let cool completely before frosting or decorating.

FIGGY SWIRL COOKIES

I admit it. There are things about baking that make me feel like a kid again. These cookies remind me of those famous fig cookies from my childhood that you can still buy at the grocery store. You knew I had to zhuzh them up, though, didn't you?

½ cup (103 g) organic palm shortening

3 tablespoons (45 ml) honey, divided

1 teaspoon organic vanilla extract

½ teaspoon finely grated orange zest

1 tablespoon (10 g) grass-fed gelatin

1 tablespoon (15 ml) water

2 tablespoons (30 ml) hot water (not boiling)

¾ cup (101 g) cassava flour, plus more as needed

½ teaspoon baking soda

½ teaspoon sea salt

¼ teaspoon cream of tartar

½ cup (75 g) chopped dried stemmed figs

2 tablespoons (30 ml) fresh orange juice

Preheat the oven to 350°F (175°C or gas mark 4). Line a baking sheet with parchment paper.

In a large bowl, cream the shortening until fluffy. Add 2 tablespoons (30 ml) of honey, the vanilla, and orange zest and cream again.

Pour 1 tablespoon (15 ml) of water into a small bowl. Sprinkle in the gelatin and whisk gently to combine. Add the hot water and whisk vigorously until frothy. Immediately add the gelatin to the shortening mixture and cream everything together.

In another large bowl, whisk the flour, baking soda, salt, and cream of tartar to blend. Add the dry ingredients to the shortening mixture and stir to form a dough. The dough should not be sticky to the touch. If the dough is too wet, add more flour, 1 tablespoon (8 g) at a time, until you get a dough that will stick well to *itself*, but not to you.

In a mini food processor or blender, combine the figs, 1 tablespoon (15 ml) of honey, and the orange juice and whirl until you have a paste.

On a piece of parchment paper, press the dough into a 5 × 7-inch (13 × 18 cm) rectangle with your hands. Spread the fig mixture over the dough, leaving a ¼ inch (6 mm) edge. Carefully roll up the dough lengthwise. If cracks appear in the dough, gently roll the log a bit to helps seal the cracks.

To cut each cookie, slide a length of baker's twine or unflavored, unwaxed dental floss under the log ½ inch (1 cm) from the top. Cross the twine, then pull the ends to slice off cookie portions without flattening the log. Place the cookies on the prepared baking sheet.

Bake for 10 minutes. Let cool. Store in an airtight container at room temperature.

ICED LEMON COOKIES

Tangy, soft, and sweet, these cookies are beautiful with afternoon tea. Wait. We don't need a reason for cookies, do we? Just enjoy them!

FOR THE COOKIES:

- ½ cup (103 g) organic palm shortening, plus more for greasing
- ¼ cup (60 ml) honey
- 1 teaspoon organic vanilla extract
- ½ teaspoon grated lemon zest
- 2 tablespoons (30 ml) fresh lemon juice
- 1 tablespoon (10 g) grass-fed gelatin
- ¾ cup (120 g) cassava flour
- ½ teaspoon baking soda
- ½ teaspoon sea salt
- ¼ teaspoon cream of tartar

FOR THE ICING:

- ½ cup (80 g) arrowroot flour
- 2 tablespoons (30 ml) fresh lemon juice
- 2 tablespoons (30 ml) water
- 2 tablespoons (30 ml) honey

Preheat the oven to 350°F (175°C or gas mark 4). Lightly grease a baking sheet with shortening.

To make the cookies: In a large bowl, cream together the shortening, honey, vanilla, and lemon zest until very fluffy.

Pour the lemon juice into a cold saucepan. Sprinkle in the gelatin and let sit for 2 minutes to "bloom." Place the saucepan over medium-low heat. Cook, gently whisking, until all the gelatin is liquified. Remove from the heat and whisk vigorously until frothy. Immediately add the gelatin to the shortening mixture and cream everything together.

In a medium-size bowl, whisk the flour, baking soda, salt, and cream of tartar to blend. Add the dry ingredients to the shortening mixture and stir to form a dough. Using a 1-tablespoon cookie scoop, drop the dough onto the prepared baking sheet (it will need two batches).

Bake for 10 minutes. Transfer to a cooling rack to cool. Repeat for the second batch.

To make the icing: In a small bowl, whisk the arrowroot, lemon juice, water, and honey until smooth.

Place the cooled cookies on a cooling rack set on a baking sheet. Spoon the icing onto each cookie, letting the excess drip onto the baking sheet. Let the icing solidify a bit before serving.

N'OREOS

These sandwich cookies bring back all sorts of memories for me. The great thing about making your own, besides being allergy friendly, is that they can be filled with any frosting you want! Mint, strawberry, chocolate, vanilla . . . whatever suits you. Remember, with sandwich cookies, you're really getting two cookies. Easy does it!

½ cup (103 g) organic palm short-ening, plus more for greasing

½ cup (72 g) coconut sugar

½ cup (69 g) cassava flour

¼ cup (28 g) arrowroot flour

¼ cup (24 g) carob powder

1 tablespoon (10 g) grass-fed gelatin

½ teaspoon baking soda

¼ teaspoon sea salt

¼ cup (60 ml) water

1 teaspoon organic vanilla extract

Frosting suggestions: Gingerbread Cake (page 102), Frosted Pumpkin Spice Cookies (page 62), or your favorite AIP frosting

Preheat the oven to 350°F (175°C or gas mark 4). Lightly coat a baking sheet with shortening.

In a large bowl, cream the shortening until fluffy. Add the coconut sugar and cream again.

In a medium-size bowl, gently whisk the cassava flour, arrowroot, carob powder, gelatin, baking soda, and salt to blend. Add the dry ingredients to the shortening mixture and stir to combine. The mixture will be pebbly. Stir in the water and vanilla.

Form a generous handful of dough into a patty. Roll it between two sheets of parchment paper to ⅛ to ¼ inch (3 to 6 mm) thick. Keep them on the thin side for a crispier cookie.

Using a 2-inch (5 cm) cookie cutter, cut out desired shapes and place them on the prepared baking sheet. Repeat with the remaining dough.

Bake for 10 minutes. Let the cookies cool completely before frosting and filling them.

Spread a thin layer of your frosting of choice on the bottom of one cookie, then place another cookie on top.

SIMPLE MAPLE CRISPS

These crispy wafers taste like those brown crispy cookies you get on an airplane—sweet and crunchy. Best of all, they are super easy to make! If you've got a hankering for a little something sweet, but don't have a lot of energy or time, whip up a batch of these.

- ½ cup (67 g) cassava flour
- 2 tablespoons (18 g) arrow-root flour
- ½ teaspoon sea salt
- ½ teaspoon ground cinnamon
- ¼ cup (60 ml) pure maple syrup
- 2 tablespoons (30 ml) extra-virgin olive oil
- 2 tablespoons (18 g) coconut sugar

Preheat the oven to 325°F (165°C or gas mark 3). Line a baking sheet with parchment paper.

In a large bowl, combine the cassava flour, arrowroot, salt, and cinnamon. Using a fork, mix in the syrup and oil. The dough will be soft and sticky, but workable.

Place the coconut sugar in a small bowl. Scoop the dough out by the teaspoonful. Roll the dough into a ball, then roll the ball in the coconut sugar and place it on the prepared baking sheet.

Place a second piece of parchment paper on top of the cookie balls. Smash each ball flat to ⅛ inch (3 mm) thick with the bottom of a measuring cup. Carefully remove the top piece of parchment only.

Bake for 15 minutes. Let cool to crisp up.

THUMBPRINT COOKIES

Yes, it is possible to bake these classic cookies! You can fill them with AIP-friendly fruit spread (check labels), apple butter, or the lemon filling I include here. They are soft and chewy, but if you like your cookies a little firmer, just refrigerate before serving.

FOR THE LEMON FILLING:

Grated zest of 1 lemon

¼ cup (60 ml) fresh lemon juice

2 tablespoons (30 ml) honey

1 tablespoon (15 ml) water

1½ teaspoons arrowroot flour

FOR THE COOKIES:

½ cup (103 g) organic palm shortening

2½ tablespoons (32 ml) honey

1 teaspoon organic vanilla extract

¼ teaspoon finely grated lemon zest

1 tablespoon (15 ml) water

2 tablespoons (30 ml) hot water (not boiling)

1 tablespoon (10 g) grass-fed gelatin

¾ cup (113 g) cassava flour

½ teaspoon baking soda

½ teaspoon sea salt

¼ teaspoon cream of tartar

5 teaspoons (25 ml) lemon filling or other AIP-friendly fruit spread (such as apple butter)

To make the lemon filling (if using): In a small saucepan over medium heat, combine the lemon zest, lemon juice, and honey. Cook until the liquid is bubbling. In a small container with a tight-fitting lid, combine the water and arrowroot. Cover and shake vigorously to blend. Whisk this slurry into the lemon mixture. Cook for about 30 seconds until the filling thickens, it will be quick, then remove from the heat.

Preheat the oven to 350°F (175°C or gas mark 4). Line a baking sheet with parchment paper.

To make the cookies: In a large bowl, cream the shortening until fluffy. Add the honey, vanilla, and lemon zest and cream again.

Pour 1 tablespoon (15 ml) of water into a small bowl. Sprinkle in the gelatin and gently whisk to incorporate. Add the hot water and whisk vigorously until frothy. Immediately add the gelatin to the shortening mixture and cream again.

In a medium-size bowl, combine the flour, baking soda, salt, and cream of tartar. Add the dry ingredients to the shortening mixture and stir to form a dough. Using a 1¼-inch (3 cm) cookie scoop, scoop the dough, roll it into balls, and place the balls on the prepared baking sheet.

Bake for 10 minutes. As soon as the cookies come out of the oven, make a depression in each one using the back of a ½-teaspoon measuring spoon. While the cookies are still warm, carefully spoon in the filling. Transfer the cookies to a cooling rack to cool before serving.

TIGERNUT BUTTER & JAM SAMMIES

If you want something decadent, here you go! But ohhh myyyy . . . approach these babies with caution and be careful with this much sugar. Eating one sammie is like eating two cookies—and condiments. Feel free to substitute any other nut or seed butter, if successfully reintroduced.

8 tablespoons (107 g) organic palm shortening, plus more for greasing

3 tablespoons (45 ml) honey

1 teaspoon organic vanilla extract

1 teaspoon apple cider vinegar

2 tablespoons (30 ml) water

1 tablespoon (10 g) grass-fed gelatin

¾ cup (120 g) cassava flour

½ teaspoon baking soda

¾ teaspoon sea salt, divided

¼ teaspoon cream of tartar

3 tablespoons (45 ml) melted organic palm shortening

¼ cup plus 1 tablespoon (39 g) tigernut flour

Fruit-only fruit spread for filling (check labels)

Preheat the oven to 350°F (175°C or gas mark 4). Lightly grease a baking sheet with shortening.

In a large bowl, cream together the shortening, honey, vanilla, and vinegar until very fluffy.

Pour the water into a cold saucepan. Sprinkle in the gelatin and let sit for 2 minutes to "bloom." Place the saucepan over medium-low heat, Cook, gently whisking, until all the gelatin is liquified. Remove from the heat and whisk vigorously until frothy. Immediately add the gelatin to the shortening mixture and cream again.

In a medium-size bowl, combine the cassava flour, baking soda, ½ teaspoon of salt, and the cream of tartar. Add the dry ingredients to the shortening mixture and stir to form a dough. Using a 1-tablespoon cookie scoop, drop the dough onto the prepared baking sheet (you may need two batches).

Bake for 10 minutes. Transfer to a cooling rack. Repeat for a second batch, if needed.

In a small bowl, stir together the melted palm shortening, tigernut flour, and remaining ¼ teaspoon of salt. When the cookies are cool, spread this tigernut butter on the bottom of a cookie. Spread fruit spread on the bottom of another cookie. Put the cookies together to make a sandwich. Repeat with the remaining cookies.

. . . .

CHAPTER 4

BARS

. . . .

The wonderful thing about bar cookies is their simplicity. Make the batter, spread it in a baking dish, and let the oven finish the job. Additionally, you have more agency over your portion size. Want just a little something sweet after a meal? Cut yourself a small square. Feeling a little decadent? Cut a slab. It's all up to you. It would be irresponsible of me to encourage the latter, but I'm telling you . . . it will be hard to resist a big ol' slab of gooey Apple Butter Bars (page 84), or, for those with successful reintroductions, Chunky Monkey Bars (page 88). Don't say I didn't warn you.

APPLE BUTTER BARS

These are soooo good. If you can't do chocolate, or you don't like carob, try these. They are ooey, gooey, delicious. You can have these bars plain, but in my opinion, the glaze is worth the extra effort.

YIELD	9 BARS
PREP	20 MINUTES (EXCLUDING GLAZE)
BAKE	20 MINUTES
COOK	5 MINUTES

FOR THE BARS:

- ½ cup (103 g) organic palm shortening, plus more for greasing (optional)
- ¼ cup (60 g) organic fruit-only apple butter (read labels)
- 2 tablespoons (30 ml) pure maple syrup
- 3 tablespoons (45 ml) water
- 1 tablespoon (10 g) grass-fed gelatin
- ½ cup (54 g) tigernut flour
- ½ cup (58 g) tapioca flour
- 1 teaspoon ground cinnamon
- ½ teaspoon baking soda
- ½ teaspoon sea salt
- ¼ teaspoon cream of tartar

FOR THE GLAZE:

- 2 tablespoons (30 ml) pure maple syrup
- 2 tablespoons (30 ml) coconut oil
- 2 tablespoons (30 ml) softened and stirred coconut butter
- 2 tablespoons (30 ml) full-fat coconut milk
- 1 teaspoon alcohol-free vanilla extract
- ½ teaspoon ground cinnamon

Preheat the oven to 350°F (175°C or gas mark 4). Grease an 8 × 8-inch (20 × 20 cm) glass pan with shortening, or line it with parchment paper.

To make the bars: In a large bowl, cream the shortening until fluffy. Add the apple butter and syrup and cream again.

Pour the water into a cold saucepan. Sprinkle in the gelatin and let sit for 2 minutes to "bloom." Place the saucepan over medium-low heat. Cook, gently whisking, just until all the gelatin has liquified. Remove from the heat, tip the saucepan, and whisk vigorously until frothy. Immediately add the gelatin to the shortening mixture and cream again.

All at once, add the flours, cinnamon, baking soda, salt, and cream of tartar to the shortening mixture and stir until thoroughly combined. Spread the batter evenly in the prepared pan.

Bake for 20 minutes. Let cool completely in the pan before glazing or serving.

To make the glaze (if using): In a small saucepan over medium-low heat, combine the syrup, coconut oil, and coconut butter. Gently whisk until fully incorporated. Add the coconut milk, vanilla, and cinnamon and cook, gently whisking, for 2 minutes. Let the glaze cool and thicken to the consistency of melted caramel. Pour the glaze over the cooled bars and spread it out with an offset spatula. Refrigerate for 20 minutes (no longer), then serve. The glaze will lighten as it solidifies.

TIGERNUT BLONDIES

Have you had a blondie? Imagine a nonchocolate, brown sugar brownie. Truly decadent! I like my blondies a little underdone and chewy. If you want yours cooked longer, do what pleases you. These bars can be customized according to your reintroductions. You can add some melted chocolate drizzle and/or chopped nuts if you have successfully reintroduced them. For the elimination phase, stick with the recipe as is.

½   cup (103 g) organic palm shortening, plus more for greasing (optional)

⅓   cup (78 ml) pure maple syrup

3   tablespoons (45 ml) water

1   tablespoon (10 g) grass-fed gelatin

1   cup (118 g) tigernut flour

½   cup (58 g) tapioca flour

½   teaspoon baking soda

½   teaspoon sea salt

¼   teaspoon cream of tartar

1   teaspoon organic vanilla extract

Preheat the oven to 350°F (175°C or gas mark 4). Grease an 8 × 8-inch (20 × 20 cm) glass pan with shortening, or line it with parchment paper.

In a large bowl, cream the shortening until fluffy. Add the syrup and cream again.

Pour the water into a cold saucepan. Sprinkle in the gelatin and let sit for 2 minutes to "bloom." Place the saucepan over medium-low heat. Cook, gently whisking, just until the gelatin is fully liquified. Remove from the heat, tip the saucepan, and whisk vigorously until frothy. Immediately add the gelatin to the shortening mixture and cream again.

In a medium-size bowl, gently whisk the flours, baking soda, salt, and cream of tartar to blend. Stir the dry ingredients into the shortening mixture. Stir in the vanilla. Press the dough evenly into the prepared pan with your hands.

Bake for 17 minutes, or longer, if you like your blondies done more. Let cool in the pan before serving.

"CHOCOLATE" SHORTBREAD

This recipe is similar to the basic Shortbread (page 92), but with more of a chocolatey flavor. It's fun to make both kinds and serve them together.

½ cup (103 g) organic palm shortening, melted

¼ cup (60 ml) pure maple syrup

1 teaspoon organic vanilla extract

¾ cup (101 g) cassava flour

¼ cup (31 g) tapioca flour

¼ cup (24 g) carob powder, plus ½ teaspoon (optional), or cocoa powder (if successfully reintroduced)

½ teaspoon baking soda

½ teaspoon sea salt

¼ teaspoon cream of tartar

¼ teaspoon ground cinnamon

½ teaspoon coconut sugar (optional)

Preheat the oven to 325°F (165°C or gas mark 3). Line an 8 × 8-inch (20 × 20 cm) glass pan with parchment paper, letting it overhang the sides.

In a large bowl, combine the shortening, syrup, vanilla, flours, ¼ cup (24 g) of carob powder, the baking soda, salt, cream of tartar, and cinnamon. Mix well with a spoon. Press the dough as evenly as possible with your hands into the prepared pan, ensuring the edges don't creep up the sides.

Bake for 25 minutes.

Meanwhile, in a small bowl, stir together the remaining ½ teaspoon of carob powder (if using) and the coconut sugar (if using).

Remove the bars from the oven and sprinkle with the carob-coconut sugar blend (if using). Let cool for 10 minutes. Using the sides of the parchment, carefully lift out the shortbread and place it on a cutting surface. Cut into 4 equal squares. Cut each square once, diagonally. This will produce 8 triangle shapes. Let cool the rest of the way before serving.

CHUNKY MONKEY BARS

Let's go a little bananas with the reintroductions, shall we? There are two in this recipe: chocolate (Stage 1) and walnuts (Stage 2). If you can't do chocolate, you could substitute carob powder. If nuts are a definite no for you, leave them out. I wanted to include a recipe that takes advantage of an expanding palette, which is what we're aiming for, after all!

FOR THE BARS:

Organic palm shortening for greasing (optional)

¾ cup (167 g) mashed ripe banana

½ cup (118 ml) extra-virgin olive oil

¼ cup (60 ml) pure maple syrup

1 teaspoon organic vanilla extract

¾ cup (99 g) cassava flour

⅓ cup (40 g) chopped walnuts (Stage 2 reintroduction; optional)

¼ cup (22 g) tigernut flour

¼ cup (22 g) cocoa powder (Stage 1 reintroduction) or carob powder

1½ teaspoons grass-fed gelatin

1 teaspoon sea salt

½ teaspoon baking soda

¼ teaspoon cream of tartar

FOR THE FROSTING:

½ cup (103 g) organic palm shortening

3 tablespoons (27 g) arrowroot flour

2 tablespoons (30 ml) full-fat coconut milk

1 tablespoon (15 ml) pure maple syrup   1 teaspoon alcohol-free vanilla extract

Banana slices for garnish (optional)

Chopped walnuts for garnish (optional)

Preheat the oven to 350°F (175°C or gas mark 4). Grease an 8 × 8-inch (20 × 20 cm) glass pan with shortening, or line it with parchment paper.

To make the bars: In a large bowl, whisk the banana, oil, syrup, and vanilla to blend. Stir in the cassava flour, walnuts (if using), tigernut flour, cocoa powder, gelatin, salt, baking soda, and cream of tartar. Spread the batter in the prepared pan.

Bake for 20 minutes. Let cool completely before frosting.

To make the frosting: In a tall mixing bowl, combine the shortening, arrowroot, coconut milk, vanilla, and syrup. Using a hand mixer fitted with a whisk attachment, whip the frosting until it resembles a thick whipped cream. Spread the frosting evenly over the cooled bars. Garnish with banana slices (if using) and walnuts (if using). Cut the bars into 9 pieces and serve.

BROWNIES

Is there anything more satisfying than sinking your teeth into a chocolatey brownie? This quick recipe uses one reintroduction—egg yolks (Stage 1). Every AIP "fudgy" brownie I've tried has been gummy or mushy, so I'm going with a "cakier" version here. You may be tempted to dig right in when they come out of the oven, but these guys need time to cool and set. Your patience will be rewarded.

Organic palm shortening for greasing (optional)

½ cup plus 2 tablespoons (148 ml) extra-virgin olive oil

2 large egg yolks (Stage 1 reintroduction)

¼ cup (36 g) coconut sugar

¼ cup (60 g) organic unsweetened applesauce

¼ cup (60 ml) water

1 teaspoon organic vanilla extract

¾ cup (99 g) cassava flour

¼ cup (22 g) tigernut flour

¼ cup (24 g) carob powder or cocoa powder (if successfully reintroduced)

1 teaspoon grass-fed gelatin

1 teaspoon sea salt

½ teaspoon baking soda

¼ teaspoon cream of tartar

Preheat the oven to 350°F (175°C or gas mark 4). Grease an 8 × 8-inch (20 × 20 cm) glass pan with shortening, or line it with parchment paper.

In a large bowl, whisk the oil, egg yolks, coconut sugar, applesauce, water, and vanilla to blend. Stir in the flours, carob powder, gelatin, salt, baking soda, and cream of tartar. Spread the batter evenly in the prepared pan.

Bake for 20 minutes. Let cool completely in the pan before cutting and serving.

VARIATION

+ Top the brownies with sliced strawberries or salted coconut cream caramel sauce and sea salt flakes.

SHORTBREAD

There's a certain mouthfeel I remember from shortbread—a little bit of snap, but also a little bit of soft—and it took me a while to achieve it. The secret turned out to be melting the shortening! It's the little things. . . .

½ cup (103 g) organic palm shortening, melted

¼ cup (60 ml) honey

1 teaspoon organic vanilla extract

¾ cup (101 g) cassava flour

½ cup (62 g) tapioca flour

½ teaspoon baking soda

½ teaspoon sea salt

¼ teaspoon cream of tartar

1½ teaspoons coconut sugar (optional)

Preheat the oven to 325°F (165°C or gas mark 3). Line an 8 × 8-inch (20 × 20 cm) glass pan with parchment paper, letting it overhang the sides.

In a large bowl, combine the shortening, honey, vanilla, flours, baking soda, salt, and cream of tartar. Mix well with a spoon. Press the dough as evenly as possible with your hands into the prepared pan, ensuring that the edges don't creep up the sides.

Bake for 25 minutes. Remove the pan from the oven and sprinkle with the coconut sugar (if using). Let cool for 10 minutes. Using the sides of the parchment, carefully lift out the shortbread and place it on a cutting surface. Cut the shortbread into 4 equal squares. Cut each square once, diagonally. This will produce 8 equal triangle shapes. Let cool the rest of the way before serving.

CHAPTER 5
CAKES

When I began working on this book, I thought for sure that cakes would be almost impossible. I'm happy to tell you I was wrong. They are totally doable! Note: You will need to follow the directions carefully on these recipes—and don't even think about substituting flours. On your next birthday celebration, try "Chocolate" Cake (page 97). Impress dinner guests with a frosted Gingerbread Cake (page 102), garnished with fresh raspberries, or Black Forest Cake (page 104) with fresh cherries. You really can do this!

"CHOCOLATE" CAKE

You will be surprised at how easy this cake is to make—and how much it behaves like the real thing! It is spongy and moist. This recipe makes one 9-inch (23 cm) cake, but here's a trick: You can make it a double-decker if you are just serving pieces without the ceremonial candle blowing. Cut the cake in half, and secure one half atop the other with frosting.

Preheat the oven to 350°F (175°C or gas mark 4). Grease a 9-inch (23 cm) cake pan with shortening and dust it with carob powder.

In a large bowl, gently whisk both flours, the carob powder, gelatin, baking soda, cream of tartar, and salt to blend.

Pour in the water, oil, and syrup. Stir to combine, ensuring there are no lumps. Add the vinegar and stir again. Scrape the batter into the prepared cake pan. Tip: Lightly jiggle the pan, side to side, on a level surface to even out the batter.

Bake for 33 minutes, or until a toothpick inserted into the center comes out clean. Let cool for 10 minutes in the pan. Loosen the cake from the sides of the pan. Place a plate or cake stand *upside-down* on the cake pan. Holding them together firmly (perhaps with oven mitts), invert. Carefully lift the cake pan from the top. Cool *completely* if you plan to frost the cake.

Organic palm shortening for greasing

¼ cup (24 g) carob powder, plus more for dusting

1½ cups (177 g) tigernut flour

½ cup (58 g) tapioca flour

1 tablespoon (10 g) grass-fed gelatin

1 teaspoon baking soda

½ teaspoon cream of tartar

½ teaspoon sea salt

¾ cup (177 ml) water

⅓ cup (78 ml) extra-virgin olive oil

⅓ cup (78 ml) pure maple syrup

1 tablespoon (15 ml) apple cider vinegar

BLUEBERRY LEMON CAKE

Dense and gooey, this unfrosted cake can work as a dessert, or as a brunch side. It's so easy! You'll have it done in less than an hour. When the cake has cooled, you might try drizzling on the icing from the Blueberry Scones (page 122) or the Raspberry Lemon Scones (page 134). Cake for allllllllll!

Organic palm shortening for greasing

1 cup (155 g) frozen blueberries

1½ cups (177 g) tigernut flour

¾ cup (87 g) tapioca flour

¾ teaspoon baking soda

½ teaspoon sea salt

¼ teaspoon cream of tartar

¼ cup (60 ml) water

1 tablespoon (10 g) grass-fed gelatin

⅓ cup (78 ml) honey

⅓ cup (78 ml) extra-virgin olive oil

Grated zest of 1 lemon

2 tablespoons (30 ml) fresh lemon juice

Preheat the oven to 350°F (175°C or gas mark 4). Grease a 9-inch (23 cm) cake pan with shortening.

In a large bowl, gently stir together the blueberries, flours, baking soda, salt, and cream of tartar.

Pour the water into a cold saucepan. Sprinkle in the gelatin and let sit for 2 minutes to "bloom." Place the saucepan over medium heat. Cook, gently whisking, until the gelatin has fully liquified. Remove from the heat, tilt the pan, and whisk vigorously until frothy. Immediately add the gelatin to the dry ingredients.

Add the honey, oil, lemon zest, and lemon juice and stir to combine. The batter will be quite thick and lumpy. Spread the batter evenly in the prepared cake pan.

Bake for 33 minutes. Cool the cake in the pan to let the gelatin set. Slice into wedges to serve.

STREUSEL COFFEE CAKE

This cake is almost not a cake, it's so moist! (My apologies to those of you who take issue with that adjective.) Growing up, it was always a treat to have streusel coffee cake from the freezer section of the grocery store. The softer, the better. My childhood dreams are presented for you here in this cake with a streusel topping and a very soft, slightly apple-y bottom layer. If you were in my house, I'd give you a slice. Instead, here's the recipe!

FOR THE COFFEE CAKE:

    Organic palm shortening for greasing (optional)
1½ cups (177 g) tigernut flour
½   cup (58 g) tapioca flour
1   tablespoon (10 g) grass-fed gelatin
1   teaspoon baking soda
½   teaspoon cream of tartar
½   teaspoon sea salt
½   teaspoon ground cinnamon
½   cup (125 g) organic unsweetened applesauce
¼   cup (60 ml) extra-virgin olive oil
¼   cup (60 ml) pure maple syrup
¼   cup (60 ml) water
1   tablespoon (15 ml) apple cider vinegar

FOR THE STREUSEL TOPPING:

½   cup (50 g) tigernut flour
⅓   cup (43 g) cassava flour
⅓   cup (68 g) organic palm shortening
¼   cup (36 g) coconut sugar
¼   cup (48 g) sliced tigernuts
½   teaspoon ground cinnamon
¼   teaspoon sea salt

Preheat the oven to 350°F (175°C or gas mark 4). Grease an 8 × 8-inch (20 × 20 cm) glass baking dish, or line it with parchment paper.

To make the cake: In a large bowl, gently whisk the flours, gelatin, baking soda, cream of tartar, salt, and cinnamon to blend. Add the applesauce, oil, syrup, and water. Stir to combine, ensuring there are no lumps. Add the vinegar and stir again. Spread the batter evenly in the prepared pan.

To make the topping: In a food processor, combine the flours, palm shortening, coconut sugar, sliced tigernuts, cinnamon, and salt and pulse until fully combined and crumbly. Spread the streusel evenly over the batter.

Bake for 33 to 35 minutes until a toothpick inserted into the center of the cake comes out clean. Let cool to set.

CARROT CAKE EVERYTHING

Carrot Cake Everything is one recipe with many possible iterations. You can make muffins, cupcakes, or go all the way with a double-decker cake. Thanks to puréed plantains and applesauce, this cake is heavy and dense, just like you expect a carrot cake to be.

FOR THE BATTER:

- ½ cup (68 g) cassava flour, plus more for dusting
- ½ cup (58 g) arrowroot flour
- ¼ cup (24 g) coconut flour
- 1 tablespoon (10 g) grass-fed gelatin
- 2 teaspoons (5 g) ground cinnamon
- 1½ teaspoons baking soda
- 1 teaspoon sea salt
- ½ teaspoon cream of tartar
- ¼ teaspoon ground ginger
- ¼ teaspoon ground cloves
- 3 cups (450 g) sliced peeled ripe plantain (from about 2 large, yellow and black)
- ½ cup (125 g) organic unsweetened applesauce
- ¼ cup (60 ml) melted organic palm shortening, plus more for greasing
- 2 tablespoons (30 ml) pure maple syrup
- 2 teaspoons (10 ml) organic vanilla extract

Preheat the oven to 350°F (175°C or gas mark 4).

To make the batter: In a large bowl, whisk the cassava flour, arrowroot, coconut flour, gelatin, cinnamon, baking soda, salt, cream of tartar, ginger, and cloves to blend.

In a food processor, combine the plantain, applesauce, melted shortening, syrup, vanilla, and molasses (if using). Process until very smooth. Add these wet ingredients to the dry ingredients, then add the carrot and raisins. Stir until all the ingredients are fully incorporated. The batter will be quite thick.

To make one cake: Grease a 9-inch (23 cm) cake pan with palm shortening and dust it with cassava flour. Pour the batter into the prepared pan. Smooth the batter with an offset spatula. Bake for 30 minutes, or until a toothpick inserted into the center of the cake comes out clean. Let cool in the pan for 10 minutes. Turn the cake out onto a cooling rack and let cool *completely* before frosting.

To make muffins: Line 13 wells of 2 standard muffin tins with silicone liners. Spoon the batter into the liners and smooth the tops with an offset spatula. Bake for 20 to 25 minutes, or until a toothpick inserted into the middle of a muffin comes out clean. Start checking at 20 minutes. Let cool in the tin for at least 10 minutes before turning the muffins out onto a cooling rack. Let cool completely so the gelatin sets.

To make cupcakes: Make muffins as described previously. Frost them and they become cupcakes! Wait until the cupcakes are *completely* cool before frosting.

¼ teaspoon organic unsul-
   fured blackstrap molasses
   (optional, for color)

½ cup (55 g) shredded carrot

½ cup (75 g) raisins

FOR THE FROSTING

½ cup (64 g) arrowroot flour

3 tablespoons (45 ml) pure
   maple syrup

1 teaspoon apple cider
   vinegar

⅛ teaspoon pure, food-grade
   lemon oil

To make a double-decker carrot cake with frosting: Double the batter recipe. Double the frosting recipe. Grease two 9-inch (23 cm) cake pans with palm shortening and dust them lightly with cassava flour. Divide the batter between the prepared pans. Smooth the batter with an offset spatula. Bake for 30 minutes, or until a toothpick inserted into the center of the cakes comes out clean. Let cool in the pans for 10 minutes. Turn the cakes out onto a cooling rack. Let cool completely before frosting.

To make the frosting: In a medium-size bowl, using a hand mixer fitted with a whisk attachment, cream the shortening until fluffy. Add the arrowroot, syrup, vinegar, and lemon oil and cream again. The frosting will be fluffy. If you'd like it to be a bit stiffer, refrigerate for 10 minutes. If it chills too long, it will harden. Gently bring it back to room temperature, stir, and it'll be fine.

GINGERBREAD CAKE

This moist and surprisingly light cake is good any time of year, but especially during holidays and cold-weather days. Topping with fresh fruit really levels it up! Who needs artificial colors to make a beautiful cake . . . ?

- ¼ cup (60 ml) melted organic palm shortening, plus more for greasing
- ½ cup (72 g) cassava flour
- ½ cup (60 g) tapioca flour
- ¼ cup (30 g) tigernut flour
- 1 tablespoon (10 g) grass-fed gelatin
- 1½ teaspoons baking soda
- 1 teaspoon sea salt
- 1 teaspoon ground ginger
- 1 teaspoon ground cloves
- ½ teaspoon ground cinnamon
- ½ teaspoon cream of tartar
- 2½ cups (375 g) sliced peeled ripe plantain (from about 2 large, yellow and black)
- ½ cup (125 g) organic unsweetened applesauce
- ¼ cup (60 ml) organic unsulfured blackstrap molasses
- 2 teaspoons (30 ml) organic vanilla extract

Preheat the oven to 350°F (175°C or gas mark 4). Grease a 9-inch (23 cm) cake pan with palm shortening.

In a large bowl, gently whisk the flours, gelatin, baking soda, salt, ginger, cloves, cinnamon, and cream of tartar to blend.

In a food processor, combine the plantain, applesauce, shortening, molasses, and vanilla. Process until very smooth, stopping to scrape down the bowl occasionally to ensure there are no lumps. Add the wet ingredients to the dry ingredients and stir well to combine. Spread the batter evenly in the prepared pan.

Bake for 30 minutes, or until a toothpick inserted into the center of the cake comes out clean. Let cool in the pan for 10 minutes. Turn the cake out onto a cake stand or plate. Let the cake cool completely before frosting or serving with fresh fruit (or both!).

To make the frosting (if using): In a large bowl, using a hand mixer fitted with a whisk attachment. cream together ½ cup (103 g) organic palm shortening, ¼ cup (32 g) arrowroot flour, 1 tablespoon (15 ml) honey, and ⅛ teaspoon food-grade lemon oil.

BLACK FOREST CAKE

This cake feels so decadent. It's hard to believe it contains no chocolate, gluten, eggs, dairy, or processed sugar. It's slightly less sweet than the traditional version, but ever so yummy!

FOR THE CAKE:

Organic palm shortening for greasing

3 tablespoons (18 g) carob powder, plus more for dusting

3 cups (450 g) sliced peeled ripe plantain (from about 2 large, yellow and black)

½ cup (120 ml) full-fat coconut milk

¼ cup (60 ml) melted coconut oil

2 tablespoons (30 ml) pure maple syrup

2 teaspoons (10 ml) organic vanilla extract

½ cup (68 g) cassava flour

½ cup (59 g) arrowroot flour

¼ cup (23 g) coconut flour

1 tablespoon (10 g) grass-fed gelatin

1 teaspoon sea salt

1½ teaspoons baking soda

½ teaspoon cream of tartar

Preheat the oven to 350°F (175°C or gas mark 4). Grease a 9-inch (23 cm) cake pan with shortening and dust it with carob powder.

To make the cake: In a food processor, combine the plantain, coconut milk, coconut oil, syrup, and vanilla. Process until very smooth.

In a large bowl, whisk the cassava flour, arrowroot, coconut flour, gelatin, salt, baking soda, carob powder, and cream of tartar to blend. Add the plantain mixture to the dry ingredients. Stir well, making sure to dig all the way to the bottom of the bowl to get all the dry ingredients incorporated. Pour the "batter" into the prepared cake pan and spread it evenly. Note: This will not look like normal cake batter. It will be quite thick.

Bake for 30 minutes, or until a toothpick inserted into the center of the cake comes out clean. Let cool.

To make the topping: Make certain there are no pits in your halved cherries. In a saucepan, combine half of the cherries with ⅓ cup (78 ml) of water and the syrup. Place the pan over medium heat. Cook, mashing the cherries with a spoon to release the cherry juice, until the liquid is a lovely, dark red, then strain out the cherry pulp with a slotted spoon and save for another use such as a smoothie or protein shake.

Move quickly on this step! In a small container with a tight-fitting lid, combine the arrowroot and remaining 1 tablespoon (15 ml) of water. Cover and shake vigorously to blend. Turn the heat under the cherry liquid to medium-high and cook until it begins to bubble. Remove the pan from the heat and stir in the arrowroot slurry. The sauce will thicken immediately. Add the remaining cherries and stir to incorporate everything.

FOR THE CHERRY TOPPING:

- 3 cups (465 g) fresh cherries, pitted and halved
- ⅓ cup (78 ml) filtered water, plus 1 tablespoon (15 ml)
- 1 tablespoon (9 g) arrowroot flour
- 1 tablespoon (15 ml) pure maple syrup

Loosen the cake from the sides of the pan. Place a plate or a cake stand upside-down over your cake pan. Holding the pan and serving plate together firmly, invert the whole thing. Gently and carefully, lift off the cake pan. Now, you have a cake on a serving dish, bottom-side up, which gives you a nice, sharp edge.

Spoon the cherry mixture on top of the cake, distributing it evenly. If desired, arrange the cherries into a design. Serve. Refrigerate leftovers.

SPICED PEAR CAKE

This cake is just lovely on the table, and it's not too difficult to make! Use ripe plantains (yellow and black). Be sure to give the cake plenty of time to cool so it can set. A gooey cake is good; a mushy one, not so much. Enjoy!

¼ cup (60 ml) melted coconut oil, plus more for greasing

2 firm pears, peeled, cored, and cut into ½-inch (1 cm) slices

6 tablespoons (90 ml) pure maple syrup, divided

1 tablespoon (7 g) ground cinnamon, divided

1 teaspoon ground cloves, divided

½ cup (70 g) cassava flour

½ cup (59 g) arrowroot flour

¼ cup (26 g) coconut flour

1 tablespoon (10 g) grass-fed gelatin

1 teaspoon sea salt

1½ teaspoons baking soda

½ teaspoon cream of tartar

3 cups (450 g) sliced peeled ripe plantain (from about 2 large, yellow and black)

½ cup (120 ml) full-fat coconut milk

2 teaspoons (30 ml) organic vanilla extract

Preheat the oven to 350°F (175°C or gas mark 4). Grease a 9-inch (23 cm) cake pan with coconut oil.

In a large bowl, combine the pears, 2 tablespoons (30 ml) of syrup, 1 teaspoon of cinnamon, and ½ teaspoon cloves.

In another large bowl, stir together the cassava flour, arrowroot, coconut flour, gelatin, salt, baking soda, cream of tartar, remaining 2 teaspoons (5 g) of cinnamon, and remaining ½ teaspoon of cloves.

In a food processor, combine the plantain, coconut milk, melted coconut oil, remaining 4 tablespoons (60 ml) of syrup, and the vanilla. Pulse until the mixture is very smooth, stopping to scrape down the bowl frequently. Add the wet ingredients to the dry ingredients and stir well to combine. Spread the batter evenly in the prepared cake pan.

Arrange the pear slices into rings on the cake, starting at the outer edge of the cake, overlapping slices, and ending in the center. Reserve the liquid from the pears. Press the pears evenly, halfway into the batter. Brush the reserved liquid over the pears on the cake.

Bake for 45 minutes. Let the cake cool for at least 1 hour to set. Slice and serve!

. . . .

CHAPTER 6
MUFFINS

. . . .

Muffins are a great way to have your cake and still stay on your healing path. They are like cake, but smaller. Muffins freeze well, so you can retrieve one from the freezer when you occasionally feel the need.

Whether sweet, like Apple Butter Muffins (page 110) or spicy, like Pumpkin Spice Muffies (page 119), I believe muffins would tell you "good morning" if they could (see Good Morning Mini Muffins, page 113). I guess they do, in their own way . . .

APPLE BUTTER MUFFINS

These soft muffins will make you forget you are on any kind of special diet. Bonus: They make your house smell heavenly while they bake!

1 cup (103 g) tigernut flour

½ cup (58 g) tapioca flour

1 teaspoon ground cinnamon

½ teaspoon baking soda

¼ teaspoon ground cloves

¼ teaspoon sea salt

¼ teaspoon cream of tartar

2 tablespoons (30 ml) water

1 tablespoon (10 g) grass-fed gelatin

¼ cup (60 ml) pure maple syrup

¼ cup (60 g) organic fruit-only apple butter (read labels)

2 tablespoons (30 ml) fresh lemon juice

¼ cup (60 ml) extra-virgin olive oil

Preheat the oven to 350°F (175°C or gas mark 4). Line 6 wells of a standard muffin tin with liners.

In a large bowl, whisk the flours, cinnamon, baking soda, cloves, salt, and cream of tartar to blend.

Pour 2 tablespoons (30 ml) of water into a cold saucepan. Sprinkle in the gelatin and let sit for 2 minutes to "bloom." Place the saucepan over medium-low heat. Cook, gently whisking, until all the gelatin has liquified. Immediately transfer to a stand mixer fitted with a whisk attachment and whisk at high speed for 30 seconds.

With the mixer running, gradually add the syrup, apple butter, and lemon juice. Pour in the oil in a small stream and mix until incorporated, stopping to scrape down the bowl, as needed.

Turn the mixer to low speed and add the dry ingredients, a little at a time. Turn the mixer to medium speed and mix until the batter is an even consistency. Turn off the mixer and remove the bowl. Portion the batter evenly among the muffin liners. A 2-inch (5 cm) ice-cream scoop works well.

Bake for 30 minutes, or until a toothpick inserted into the center of a muffin comes out clean. Let the muffins cool for 10 minutes in the tin before removing them, then let cool completely so the gelatin sets.

GOOD MORNING MINI MUFFINS

These little muffins will wake you up with the fragrance of orange, a perfect accompaniment to your Sunday brunch. They are soft, light, and totally nom-worthy.

- 1 cup (103 g) tigernut flour
- ½ cup (58 g) tapioca flour
- ½ teaspoon baking soda
- ¼ teaspoon sea salt
- ¼ teaspoon cream of tartar
  Grated zest of 1 orange
- 6 tablespoons (90 ml) water, divided
- 1 tablespoon (10 g) grass-fed gelatin
- ¼ cup (36 g) coconut sugar
- 2 tablespoon (30 ml) fresh orange juice
- ½ teaspoon (2 ml) organic vanilla extract
- ¼ cup (60 ml) extra-virgin olive oil

Preheat the oven to 350°F (175°C or gas mark 4). Line a mini muffin tin with parchment or silicone liners.

In a large bowl, whisk the flours, baking soda, salt, cream of tartar, and orange zest to blend.

Pour 2 tablespoons (30 ml) of water into a cold saucepan. Sprinkle in the gelatin and let sit for 2 minutes to "bloom." Place the saucepan over medium-low heat. Cook, gently whisking, until the gelatin has fully liquified, ensuring there are no lumps. Immediately transfer to a stand mixer fitted with a whisk attachment and whisk at medium-high speed until it is frothy. (A hand mixer with regular attachments may be used, but it doesn't work as well.)

With the mixer running, gradually add the coconut sugar, orange juice, and vanilla. Pour in the oil in a small stream and mix until incorporated.

Turn the mixer to its lowest setting. In batches, add the dry ingredients, stopping to scrape down the bowl, as needed. The mixture will be crumbly. Gradually add the remaining 4 tablespoons (60 ml) of water. By the tablespoonful, spoon the batter into the prepared mini muffin tin.

Bake for 20 minutes, or until a toothpick inserted into the center of a muffin comes out clean. Let the muffins cool for 5 minutes before removing them from the tin. Let cool completely before serving.

BLUEBERRY MUFFINS

These blueberry muffins are a perfect treat for a special breakfast. They may look darker in color than you're used to but are they ever delicious. Working with gelatin as a binder differs from using eggs, so follow the directions carefully. You can use a hand mixer with regular beater attachments, but a stand mixer works much better.

1   cup (103 g) tigernut flour

½   cup (58 g) tapioca flour

½   teaspoon baking soda

¼   teaspoon sea salt

¼   teaspoon cream of tartar

6   tablespoons (90 ml) water, divided

1   tablespoon (10 g) grass-fed gelatin

¼   cup (36 g) coconut sugar

2   tablespoons (30 ml) fresh lemon juice

½   teaspoon (2 ml) organic vanilla extract

¼   cup (60 ml) extra-virgin olive oil

¾   cup (116 g) frozen blueberries, not thawed

Preheat the oven to 350°F (175°C or gas mark 4). Line 6 wells of a standard muffin tin with liners.

In a large bowl, whisk the flours, baking soda, salt, and cream of tartar to blend.

Pour 2 tablespoons (30 ml) of water into a cold saucepan. Sprinkle in the gelatin and let sit for 2 minutes to "bloom." Place the saucepan over medium-low heat. Cook, gently whisking, until the gelatin has fully liquified, ensuring there are no lumps. Immediately transfer to a stand mixer fitted with a whisk attachment and whisk at high speed for 30 seconds.

Turn the mixer speed to medium-high. With the mixer running, gradually add the coconut sugar, lemon juice, and vanilla. Pour in the oil in a small stream and mix until incorporated, stopping to scrape down the bowl, as needed. The gelatin may begin to cool and stick to the side of the bowl. This is normal.

Turn the mixer to low speed and add the dry ingredients a little at a time. Stop to scrape down the bowl, as needed. The mixture may be crumbly. Gradually add the remaining 4 tablespoons (60 ml) of water and mix until the batter has an even consistency.

Turn off the mixer and remove the bowl. Stir in the frozen blueberries. Do this quickly as the gelatin in the batter will begin to stiffen. Spoon the thick batter evenly among the liners. An ice-cream scoop works well.

Bake for 30 minutes, or until a toothpick inserted into the center of a muffin comes out clean of batter. Blueberry juice is okay. Let the muffins cool for 10 minutes in the tin before removing them, then let them cool completely before serving. This is important. The gelatin in the muffins needs time to cool and set.

YIELD: 8 MUFFINS
PREP: 20 MINUTES
BAKE: 20 MINUTES

"CORN BREAD" MUFFINS

The two biggest challenges in creating any AIP baking recipe, in my opinion, are taste and texture. It's hard to hit both at the same time. And corn bread? Without, you know, corn? That's a challenge, but this recipe will fool your brain into thinking it's corn bread. Try it with some AIP chili for a real treat.

- 1 cup (150 g) sliced peeled green plantain
- ¼ cup (31 g) cassava flour
- ¼ cup (28 g) tigernut flour
- ¼ cup (26 g) coconut flour
- ¼ cup (60 ml) extra-virgin olive oil
- ¼ cup (60 ml) honey
- ¼ cup (60 ml) full-fat coconut milk
- ¼ cup (60 ml) water
- 1½ teaspoons grass-fed gelatin
- 1 teaspoon sea salt
- ¾ teaspoon baking soda
- 1 tablespoon (15 ml) apple cider vinegar

Preheat the oven to 350°F (175°C or gas mark 4). Line 8 wells of a standard muffin tin with paper or silicone liners (preferably silicone).

In a food processor, combine the plantain, flours, oil, honey, coconut milk, water, gelatin, salt, and baking soda. Add the vinegar last. Process until the batter is even and smooth. Divide the batter evenly among the liners. Wet your fingers and smooth the tops.

Bake for 20 minutes, or until a toothpick inserted into the center of a muffin comes out clean. Let cool completely to set before serving.

BANANA NUT MUFFINS

For those of you venturing into the world of reintroductions, here's a recipe you might try. Two reintroductions are required: egg yolk (Stage 1) and walnuts (Stage 2). The muffins tend to stick to paper liners because there is relatively little fat in them. For best results, use silicone liners.

1   cup (225 g) mashed ripe banana

1   large egg yolk (Stage 1 reintroduction)

2   tablespoons (30 ml) pure maple syrup

¼   cup (39 g) cassava flour

¼   cup (32 g) arrowroot flour

¼   cup (31 g) tigernut flour

1   teaspoon baking soda

½   teaspoon sea salt

¼   teaspoon cream of tartar

1   teaspoon apple cider vinegar

⅓   cup (40 g) chopped walnuts (Stage 2 reintroduction)

Preheat the oven to 350°F (175°C or gas mark 4). Line 8 wells of a standard muffin tin with silicone liners.

In a large bowl, stir together the banana, egg yolk, and syrup.

In a medium-size bowl, whisk the flours, baking soda, salt, and cream of tartar to blend. Add the dry ingredients to the banana mixture and stir. Add the vinegar and walnuts and stir again. Spoon the batter equally into the liners.

Bake for 25 minutes, or until a toothpick inserted into the center of a muffin comes out clean. Let cool in the muffin tin before removing the muffins from the liners.

PUMPKIN SPICE MUFFIES

This is the kind of muffin top you actually want! I used to love the pumpkin muffies at a certain bakery restaurant chain, and I've recreated them for us here. These pillowy muffies are soft, warm, and spiced—perfect for a midmorning snack or an autumn treat.

Organic palm shortening for greasing

1 cup (103 g) tigernut flour

½ cup (58 g) tapioca flour

½ teaspoon baking soda

½ teaspoon ground cinnamon

¼ teaspoon ground ginger

¼ teaspoon ground cloves

¼ teaspoon sea salt

¼ teaspoon cream of tartar

⅛ teaspoon ground mace

4 tablespoons (60 ml) water, divided

1 tablespoon (10 g) grass-fed gelatin

¼ cup (36 g) coconut sugar

¼ cup (61 g) pumpkin purée

½ teaspoon (2 ml) organic vanilla extract

¼ cup (60 ml) extra-virgin olive oil

Preheat the oven to 350°F (175°C or gas mark 4). Lightly grease a baking sheet with shortening.

In a large bowl, gently whisk the flours, baking soda, cinnamon, ginger, cloves, salt, cream of tartar, and mace to blend.

Pour 2 tablespoons (30 ml) of water into a cold saucepan. Sprinkle in the gelatin and let sit for 2 minutes to "bloom." Place the saucepan over medium-low heat. Cook, gently whisking, until all the gelatin has liquified, ensuring there are no lumps. Immediately transfer to a stand mixer fitted with a whisk attachment and whisk at medium-high speed for 30 seconds

With the mixer running, gradually add the coconut sugar, pumpkin, and vanilla. Pour in the oil in a small stream and mix until incorporated, stopping to scrape down the bowl, as needed.

Turn the mixer to low speed and add the dry ingredients a little at a time. Stop to scrape down bowl, as needed. Turn the mixer to medium-high speed. Gradually add the remaining 2 tablespoons (30 ml) of water and mix until the batter is an even consistency. Turn off the mixer and remove the bowl. Using a 2-inch (5 cm) trigger-release ice-cream scoop, make 8 equal dollops on the prepared baking sheet.

Bake for 20 minutes, or until a toothpick inserted into the center of a muffie comes out clean. Let the muffies cool on the baking sheet before serving.

Honey Biscuits, page 129

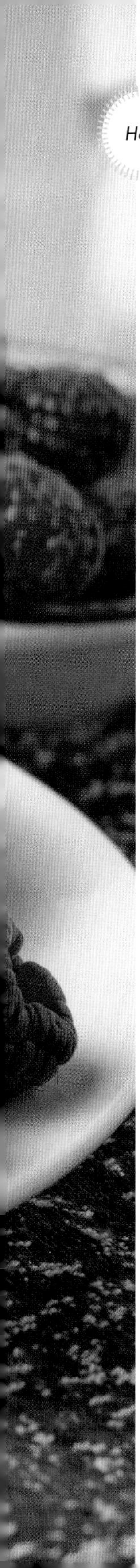

CHAPTER 7

BISCUITS & SCONES

Biscuits and scones are fun accompaniments to breakfast or brunch. I was surprised to find that they are also farthest from the tastes and textures we are accustomed to in traditional baking, in my opinion.

AIP bakers are always balancing between moisture and cohesiveness, which is a real tight-rope walk, especially for biscuits and scones. I find it helpful to remember that these are not flaky buttermilk biscuits, but AIP creations. I drizzle on some honey, and all is well. There is, however, lots of variety in this category. Try French Onion Drop Biscuits (page 128) with a bowl of soup, some Blueberry Scones (page 122) with your breakfast, or Cranberry Orange Biscotti (page 125) with your cuppa!

BLUEBERRY SCONES

When you want a brunch treat, something just a little sweet but not too much, blueberry scones will do the trick! For this recipe, the blueberries need to be frozen—unless you want them to squish when you press them.

FOR THE SCONES:

- ½ **cup (103 g) organic palm shortening, plus more for greasing**
- 1 **cup (140 g) cassava flour, plus more for dusting**
- ¼ **cup (22 g) tigernut flour**
- 1 **tablespoon (10 g) grass-fed gelatin**
- 2 **teaspoons (6 g) cream of tartar**
- ¼ **teaspoon sea salt**
- ¼ **cup (60 ml) honey**
- 2 **tablespoons (30 ml) water**
- 2 **tablespoons (30 ml) apple cider vinegar**
- ½ **cup (78 g) frozen blueberries**

FOR THE DRIZZLE:
(OPTIONAL)

- ¼ **cup (39 g) frozen blueberries**
- 4 **tablespoons (60 ml) water, divided**
- 1 **tablespoon (15 ml) pure maple syrup**
- ½ **tablespoon (5 g) arrow-root flour**

Preheat the oven to 400°F (200°C or gas mark 6). Lightly grease a baking sheet with shortening.

To make the scones: In a large bowl, gently whisk the flours, gelatin, cream of tartar, and salt to blend. Cut in the shortening with a pastry blender until everything is fully incorporated and "pebbly."

Add the honey, water, and vinegar. Mix thoroughly with a fork. Lightly dust a clean work surface and your hands with flour and gather the dough, then divide it in half. Place half the dough on the floured surface and press and form it into a disk ½ inch (1 cm) thick, with one hand on top and the other on the side to prevent cracking. Sprinkle half of the blueberries on top and press them into the dough.

Make an identical disk with the other half of the dough and press it on top of the first disk. Press the remaining berries into the top of the dough. Cut the double-decker disk into 6 equal pieces. Place the scones on the prepared baking sheet.

Bake for 13 to 15 minutes, depending on how crisp you like your scones. Let the scones cool completely on the baking sheet to set.

To make the drizzle (if using): In a small saucepan over medium-high heat, heat the blueberries, 3 tablespoons (45 ml) of water, and syrup. Cook for about 5 minutes, mashing the berries as they cook, until the liquid is dark purple. Strain the liquid into a bowl through a fine-mesh sieve. Save the blueberries for a smoothie or protein shake.

In a small container with a tight-fitting lid, combine the remaining 1 tablespoon (15 ml) of water and the arrowroot. Cover and shake vigorously to blend. Whisk this slurry into the hot blueberry liquid. Let it cool to the consistency of melted chocolate. Drizzle onto the cooled scones.

"CHEESY" BACON DROP BISCUITS

Though nutritional yeast will never be the same as real cheese, we can use it to suggest the flavor. In my opinion, it doesn't play well with sweetness, so rather than using honey or jelly on these biscuits, I suggest eating them plain, or with a slather of ghee, if you've successfully reintroduced it.

- 2   AIP-friendly bacon slices
- 1   cup (140 g) cassava flour
- ½   cup (58 g) tapioca flour
- 1½ teaspoons grass-fed gelatin
- ¼   cup (20 g) large-flake nutritional yeast
- 1   teaspoon baking soda
- ½   teaspoon cream of tartar
- ¼   teaspoon sea salt
- ½   cup (103 g) organic palm shortening
- ¾   cup (180 ml) full-fat coconut milk
- 1   tablespoon (15 ml) apple cider vinegar

Preheat the oven to 350°F (175°C or gas mark 4). Line a baking sheet with parchment paper.

In a skillet over medium heat, fry the bacon, turning frequently, until very crispy. Transfer to a plate. When the bacon is cool enough to handle, break it into small pieces.

In a large bowl, combine the flours, gelatin, nutritional yeast, baking soda, cream of tartar, and salt. Cut in the shortening with a pastry blender until it is an even consistency. Add the bacon pieces, coconut milk, and vinegar. Mix thoroughly with a fork. Scoop 8 equal portions of dough onto the prepared baking sheet.

Bake for 18 minutes. Let cool to set.

YIELD : 12 BISCOTTI
PREP : 25 MINUTES
BAKE : 27 MINUTES

CRANBERRY ORANGE BISCOTTI

Need something for munching or dunking? You can make these biscotti as crunchy as you like, but I prefer mine with just a little give to them. These biscotti will crunch more on the second day as they dry naturally, if that's your preference. Either way, they have a lovely essence.

- ¾ cup (102 g) cassava flour
- ½ cup (54 g) tigernut flour
- 1½ teaspoons grass-fed gelatin
- ½ teaspoon baking soda
- ½ teaspoon ground cinnamon
- ½ teaspoon cream of tartar
- ¼ teaspoon sea salt
- ½ cup (103 g) organic palm shortening
- ⅓ cup (40 g) dried cranberries (no added oils or sugars)
- Finely grated zest of 1 orange
- ¼ cup (60 ml) pure maple syrup
- ¼ cup (60 ml) fresh orange juice

Preheat the oven to 350°F (175°C or gas mark 4). Line a baking sheet with parchment paper.

In a large bowl, gently whisk the flours, gelatin, baking soda, cinnamon, cream of tartar, and salt to blend. Cut in the shortening with a pastry blender until the mixture is even and pebbly. Quickly stir in the cranberries, orange zest, syrup, and orange juice with a fork. The dough will be sticky.

Wet your hands and bring the dough together. Place the dough on the prepared baking sheet and form it into a 5 × 7-inch (13 × 18 cm) rectangle.

Bake for 20 minutes. Remove from the oven.

Using a very sharp knife, cut 12 strips, roughly ½ inch (1 cm) wide, and separate them with the knife on the baking sheet, leaving at least ½ inch (1 cm) of space between them. Be careful! The baking sheet is hot!

Turn the oven temperature to 300°F (150°C or gas mark 2).

Bake the strips for 7 minutes, or longer if a crunchier biscotti is desired. Let cool completely before serving.

CINNAMON RAISIN BISCUITS

These mildly sweet and rustic biscuits are best served warm right out of the oven. Try slathering them with some apple butter. If they start to dry out, just pop them in the microwave for 10 seconds.

- 1 **cup (140 g) cassava flour**
- ½ **cup (58 g) arrowroot flour**
- 1½ **teaspoons grass-fed gelatin**
- 1½ **teaspoons ground cinnamon**
- 1 **teaspoon baking soda**
- ½ **teaspoon cream of tartar**
- ¼ **teaspoon sea salt**
- ½ **cup (103 g) organic palm shortening**
- ½ **cup (75 g) raisins**
- ¼ **cup (60 g) organic unsweetened applesauce**
- ¼ **cup (60 ml) pure maple syrup**
- 1 **tablespoon (15 ml) apple cider vinegar**

Preheat the oven to 350°F (175°C or gas mark 4). Line a baking sheet with parchment paper.

In a large bowl, combine the cassava flour, arrowroot, gelatin, cinnamon, baking soda, cream of tartar, and salt. Cut in the shortening with a pastry blender until the mixture comes together evenly in pebbly, pea-size pieces. If you aren't sure you've cut it in enough, keep going.

Add the raisins, applesauce, syrup, and vinegar. Toss quickly with a fork to incorporate fully. Using a large spoon, scoop 8 equal blobs of dough onto the baking sheet. Form them a bit with your hands to make them round, and about 1¼ inches (3 cm) tall. Don't worry about getting them perfect. They're "rustic!"

Bake for 20 minutes. Serve as soon as possible.

FRENCH ONION DROP BISCUITS

These unique and savory biscuits are happiest next to hearty soups or stews. They smell and taste like French onion soup! When caramelizing onions, cook them low and slow. Like most things, they are much better when they are not hurried.

- 2 tablespoons (30 ml) extra-virgin olive oil
- 1 cup (160 g) finely chopped onion
- 2 drops of honey, plus ¼ cup (60 ml)
- 1 cup (140 g) cassava flour
- ½ cup (58 g) arrowroot flour
- 1½ teaspoons grass-fed gelatin
- 1 teaspoon baking soda
- 1 teaspoon dried thyme
- ½ teaspoon cream of tartar
- ¼ teaspoon sea salt
- ½ cup (103 g) organic palm shortening
- ¼ cup (60 ml) bone broth
- 1 tablespoon (15 ml) apple cider vinegar

In a small saucepan over medium-low heat, combine the oil, onion, and 2 drops of honey to assist with caramelizing the onions. Simmer slowly, stirring occasionally, until the onion is deep brown, but not burnt. Do not rush. Set aside to cool.

While the onion cooks, preheat the oven to 350°F (175°C or gas mark 4). Line a baking sheet with parchment paper.

In a large bowl, combine the cassava flour, arrowroot, gelatin, baking soda, thyme, cream of tartar, and salt. Cut in the shortening with a pastry blender until the mixture comes together in pea-size pieces. Add the onion, remaining ¼ cup (60 ml) of honey, the broth, and vinegar. Mix thoroughly with a fork. Using a large spoon, scoop 9 equal portions of dough onto the prepared baking sheet.

Bake for 15 minutes. Let cool so the gelatin sets.

HONEY BISCUITS

These honey biscuits are quite versatile! If you've made some AIP sausage, these are wonderful for making breakfast sandwiches. Of course, they are just as delicious with a slather of ghee (if reintroduced) or a drizzle of honey.

1   cup plus 2 tablespoons (169 g) cassava flour

½   cup (63 g) arrowroot flour

1½ teaspoons grass-fed gelatin

1½ teaspoons baking soda

½   teaspoon cream of tartar

¼   teaspoon sea salt

½   cup (103 g) organic palm shortening

½   cup (120 ml) full-fat coconut milk, plus 1 tablespoon (15 ml; optional)

2   tablespoons (30 ml) honey, plus 1 teaspoon (optional)

1   tablespoon (15 ml) apple cider vinegar

Preheat the oven to 425°F (220°C or gas mark 7).

In a large bowl, gently whisk the cassava flour, arrowroot, gelatin, baking soda, cream of tartar, and salt to blend. Cut in the shortening with a pastry blender until the mixture begins to come together in pea-size pieces.

In a small bowl, whisk ½ cup (120 ml) of coconut milk, 2 tablespoons (30 ml) of honey, and the vinegar to combine. Pour the wet ingredients into the dry ingredients and mix quickly with a fork.

Gather the dough together into a ball. Place the dough on a piece of parchment paper and press it into a disk about 1¼ inches (3 cm) thick. Cut the dough into 6 equal parts with a knife or use a 2½-inch (6 cm)-diameter biscuit cutter. Place the biscuits on an ungreased baking sheet.

If desired, in a small cup, stir together the remaining 1 tablespoon (15 ml) of coconut milk and remaining 1 teaspoon of honey and brush the mixture on the biscuits.

Bake for 7 minutes. Without opening the oven door, turn the oven temperature to 350°F (175°C or gas mark 4) and bake for 3 minutes more. Let the biscuits cool on the baking sheet for 5 to 10 minutes to set before serving.

SWEET POTATO BACON BREAKFAST CAKES

These breakfast cakes are half biscuit, half oven fritter. They do contain one reintroduction, egg yolks (Stage 1). They are best served fresh from the oven with a drizzle of pure maple syrup on top. These contain bacon, egg, and sweet potato—add a little fruit or sauerkraut on the side and call it breakfast!

- ½ cup (55 g) petite diced sweet potato
- 3 AIP-friendly bacon slices
- ¾ cup (130 g) cassava flour
- ½ cup (58 g) arrowroot flour
- 1 teaspoon baking soda
- ½ teaspoon cream of tartar
- ¼ teaspoon sea salt
- ½ cup (103 g) organic palm shortening
- ¼ cup (60 ml) pure maple syrup, plus more for serving
- 1½ tablespoons (22 ml) apple cider vinegar
- 2 large egg yolks (Stage 1 reintroduction)

Fit a saucepan with a steamer basket and fill it with water just until the water touches the basket. Place the saucepan over medium-high heat. Place the sweet potato in the basket, cover, and steam for about 10 minutes until the sweet potato is quite soft. Set aside to cool.

While the sweet potato steams, in a 10-inch (26 cm) cast-iron skillet over medium heat, cook the bacon, turning occasionally, until crispy. Transfer the bacon to a plate but reserve the bacon grease in the skillet. Turn the heat under the skillet to low to keep the pan warm.

Preheat the oven to 350°F (175°C or gas mark 4).

In a large bowl, combine the cassava flour, arrowroot, baking soda, cream of tartar, and salt. Cut in the shortening with a pastry blender until the mixture comes together in pea-size pieces.

In another bowl, mash the cooled sweet potato well with a fork. Add the syrup and vinegar to the bowl, stir until well combined, and add the sweet potato to the flour mixture. Crumble the bacon and add it along with the egg yolks. Toss everything together quickly with a fork. Drop the dough into the warm skillet in twelve 2-inch (5 cm) scoops. An ice-cream scoop works well.

Place the skillet in the oven and bake for 20 minutes. Serve immediately. Scoop the cakes onto each plate and drizzle with syrup.

MAPLE SWEET POTATO BISCUITS

These petite biscuits are sweet enough that they need no additional condiments. They are small enough, too, that you won't need to cut them. Just bite into these soft little pillows. Best served warm.

½ cup (55 g) petite diced sweet potato

¾ cup (130 g) cassava flour

½ cup (58 g) arrowroot flour

1 teaspoon baking soda

½ teaspoon cream of tartar

¼ teaspoon sea salt

½ cup (103 g) organic palm shortening

¼ cup (60 g) organic unsweetened applesauce

¼ cup (60 ml) pure maple syrup

1 tablespoon (15 ml) apple cider vinegar

Preheat the oven to 350°F (175°C or gas mark 4).

Fit a saucepan with a steamer basket and fill the pan with water just until it touches the basket. Place the saucepan over medium-high heat. Place the sweet potato in the basket, cover, and steam for about 10 minutes until the sweet potato is quite soft. Set aside to cool.

In a large bowl, combine the cassava flour, arrowroot, baking soda, cream of tartar, and salt. Cut in the shortening with a pastry blender until the mixture comes together almost like dough.

In another bowl, mash the cooled sweet potato well with a fork. Add the applesauce, syrup, and vinegar. Stir until well combined. Add the wet ingredients to the dry ingredients. Toss quickly and thoroughly with a fork. The dough will be sticky. Drop the dough in dollops, slightly less than ¼ cup (35 g) each, onto an ungreased baking sheet. A 2-inch (5 cm) trigger-release ice-cream scoop works perfectly.

Bake for 20 minutes. Let the biscuits cool for 5 minutes on the baking sheet to set. Serve warm.

RASPBERRY LEMON SCONES

Well, this one was challenging. Did you know that raspberries, being acidic, react with baking soda and turn blue on the edges, looking moldy? Me, neither. I discovered that cream of tartar, as the leavener, and a little extra acid in the dough keeps this from happening! For this recipe, the raspberries need to be frozen. Fresh fruit is too delicate.

FOR THE SCONES:

- 1 cup (140 g) cassava flour, plus more for dusting
- ¼ cup (23 g) coconut flour
- ¼ cup (36 g) coconut sugar
- 1 tablespoon (10 g) grass-fed gelatin
- 2 teaspoons (6 g) cream of tartar
- ¼ teaspoon sea salt
- ½ cup (103 g) organic palm shortening
- ¼ cup (60 ml) full-fat coconut milk
- Grated zest of 1 lemon
- ¼ cup (60 ml) fresh lemon juice
- ½ cup (125 g) frozen raspberries

FOR THE DRIZZLE:

- ¼ cup (60 ml) full-fat coconut milk
- 1 tablespoon (15 ml) pure maple syrup
  1 tablespoon (15 ml) fresh lemon juice
- 1 tablespoon (15 ml) water, plus more as needed
- 1 tablespoon (9 g) arrowroot flour

Preheat the oven to 400°F (200°C or gas mark 6). Line a baking sheet with parchment paper.

To make the scones: In a large bowl, gently whisk the flours, coconut sugar, gelatin, cream of tartar, and salt to blend. Cut in the shortening with a pastry blender until it resembles coarse cornmeal and everything is fully incorporated.

Add the coconut milk, lemon zest, and lemon juice. Mix quickly and thoroughly with a fork. Dust a clean work surface and your hands with flour and gather the dough, then divide it in half. Place the dough on the floured surface and press and form it into a disk ½ inch (1 cm) thick, with one hand on top and the other on the side to prevent cracking.

Sprinkle half of the raspberries on top of the dough and press them into the dough. Make an identical disk with the other half of dough and press it on top of the first disk. Press the remaining raspberries into the top of the dough. Cut the double-decker disk into 6 equal pieces. Place the scones on the prepared baking sheet.

Bake for 13 minutes. Let cool completely to set.

To make the drizzle: In a small microwave-safe bowl or a small saucepan, whisk all the drizzle ingredients. Heat just until thickened. For the bowl, microwave for 45 to 60 seconds. For the saucepan, heat over medium-high heat. If the drizzle gets too thick, whisk in a bit more water. Drizzle onto the cooled scones.

· · · · · · · · · · · · · · · ·

CHAPTER 8

CRISPS, CRUMBLES & COBBLERS

· · · · · · · · · · · · · · · ·

This group of recipes will gladden your heart. Fruit is fruit, AIP or not. And we can have crisps, crumbles, and cobblers that are quite reminiscent of the non-AIP versions. Fruited desserts also offer nutrients, even as we are fulfilling our desire for something sweet.

The toppings are what define this style of dessert. Crisps, like Rhubarb Crisp (page 141), generally have a crispy topping. Crumbles, like Spiced Peach Crumble (page 143), have a pebbly topping that may not crisp all the way. Cobblers, like Blueberry Cobbler (page 138), have a much thicker topping, sometimes like a biscuit. I'm a big fan of crisp toppings, and I *might* possibly overdo it sometimes. I leave it to you to decide the precise amount of topping you like on your dessert.

BLUEBERRY COBBLER

Once upon a time, a blueberry pie filling and some biscuits got together, and they were amazing. The end. *Okay, maybe there is a bit more to the story.* There are many ingredients to this dessert, but the actual making of it is easy, which is more than I can say for most AIP baking! Food styling skills are not necessary. Just plop the biscuit dough in clumps on the filling and bake. The end. Really.

FOR THE FILLING:

- 4 cups (620 g) fresh or frozen blueberries
- ¼ cup (60 ml) honey
- Grated zest of 1 lemon
- ¼ teaspoon sea salt
- ¼ teaspoon ground cinnamon
- 3 tablespoons (27 g) arrowroot flour
- 2 tablespoons (30 ml) fresh lemon juice

FOR THE TOPPING:

- 1 cup (140 g) cassava flour
- ½ cup (58 g) tapioca flour
- 1½ teaspoons grass-fed gelatin
- 1 teaspoon baking soda
- ½ teaspoon cream of tartar
- ½ teaspoon ground cinnamon
- ½ teaspoon sea salt
- ⅓ cup (68 g) organic palm shortening
- ¼ cup (60 ml) pure maple syrup
- ¼ cup (60 ml) full-fat coconut milk
- 1 tablespoon (15 ml) apple cider vinegar

Preheat the oven to 350°F (175°C or gas mark 4).

To make the filling: In a large saucepan over medium heat, combine all the filling ingredients. Cook for 5 to 10 minutes, stirring and mashing about half the berries, until the mixture is dark purple and thickened. Transfer to an ungreased 8 × 8-inch (20 × 20 cm) glass baking dish.

To make the topping: In a food processor, combine all the topping ingredients. Pulse until evenly incorporated into a dough, stopping to scrape down the bowl, as needed. Arrange the dough in small, random dollops over the blueberry mixture, leaving spaces for berries to peek through. Press the dough lightly into the filling.

Bake for 15 minutes. Let cool completely so the gelatin sets.

CHERRY COBBLER

If we're going to have a treat, why not use ingredients with some nutritive benefit? Cherries! This "bougie" version of an old-fashioned recipe uses frozen cherries, making it possible year-round. The topping uses mashed ripe plantain. For best results, choose plantains that are yellow and black and process them in a food processor.

4 cups (454 g) frozen pitted cherries

⅓ cup (78 ml) honey

2 tablespoons (30 ml) fresh lemon juice

2 tablespoons (18 g) arrow-root flour

1 teaspoon balsamic vinegar

½ cup (113 g) mashed ripe plantain

¾ cup (67 ml) tigernut flour

½ cup (56 g) tapioca flour

¼ cup (60 ml) extra-virgin olive oil

¼ cup (60 ml) pure maple syrup

¾ teaspoon baking soda

½ teaspoon sea salt

½ teaspoon ground cinnamon

Preheat the oven to 350°F (175°C or gas mark 4).

In an 8 × 8-inch (20 × 20 cm) baking dish or 8-inch (20 cm) round casserole, stir together the cherries, honey, lemon juice, arrowroot, and vinegar. The mixture will be sticky.

In a large bowl, thoroughly stir together the plantain, flours, oil, syrup, baking soda, salt, and cinnamon. Spoon dollops of batter over the cherries, allowing places for the cherries to peek through.

Bake for 40 to 50 minutes until the center is fairly set. Let cool completely to set before serving.

RECIPE IMAGE APPEARS ON PAGE 14.

YIELD : 6 SERVINGS
PREP : 35 MINUTES
BAKE : 20 MINUTES

PEAR CRUMBLE

This crumble is milder than the Spiced Peach Crumble (page 143) and would be wonderful after a delicate dish, such as a salad or a light fish. I'm using Bosc pears rather than the typical Bartlett variety because they hold up to heat better and won't turn to mush.

- 4 cups (560 g) sliced peeled, cored Bosc pears
- ⅓ cup (78 ml) water, plus 1 tablespoon (15 ml)
- 1 tablespoon (15 ml) unsweetened apple juice
- 1 tablespoon (15 ml) honey
- 1 teaspoon organic vanilla extract
- ¾ teaspoon sea salt, divided
- 1 teaspoon ground cinnamon, divided
- ¼ teaspoon ground ginger
- ⅛ teaspoon ground mace
- 1 tablespoon (9 g) arrowroot flour
- ½ cup (50 g) tigernut flour
- ⅓ cup (43 g) cassava flour
- ⅓ cup (68 g) organic palm shortening
- ¼ cup (36 g) coconut sugar
- ¼ cup (24 g) sliced tigernuts

Preheat the oven to 350°F (175°C or gas mark 4).

In a large saucepan over medium heat, combine the pears, ⅓ cup (78 ml) of water, the apple juice, honey, vanilla, ½ teaspoon of salt, ½ teaspoon of cinnamon, ginger, and mace.

Heat for 7 minutes, stirring.

In a small container with a tight-fitting lid, combine the arrowroot and remaining 1 tablespoon (15 ml) of water. Cover and shake vigorously to blend. Add this slurry to the pears and cook for about 30 seconds until thickened. Spread the fruit mixture evenly in the bottom of an ungreased 8 × 8-inch (20 × 20 cm) glass pan.

In a food processor, combine the flours, shortening, coconut sugar, sliced tigernuts, remaining ¼ teaspoon of salt, and remaining ½ teaspoon of cinnamon. Process until everything is combined and crumbly. Spread the topping evenly over the fruit mixture.

Bake for 20 minutes. Let cool completely to set before serving.

YIELD : 6 SERVINGS
PREP : 25 MINUTES
BAKE : 45 MINUTES

RHUBARB CRISP

This nostalgic summer treat gets an AIP re-vamp. Rhubarb can be overlooked as (technically) a vegetable to eat, but I like it. If you grow it, please don't eat the poisonous leaves! Just use the stalks.

- 3½ cups (427 g) diced fresh rhubarb
- ½ cup (120 ml) honey
- 1 tablespoon (9 g) arrow-root flour
- 1 tablespoon (15 ml) fresh lemon juice
- ⅛ teaspoon sea salt, plus ¼ teaspoon
- ¾ cup (75 g) tigernut flour
- ½ cup (75 g) cassava flour
- ½ cup (103 g) organic palm shortening
- ¼ cup (36 g) coconut sugar
- ½ teaspoon ground cinnamon
- ½ cup (48 g) sliced tigernuts

Preheat the oven to 350°F (175°C or gas mark 4).

In a large bowl, toss together the rhubarb, honey, arrowroot, lemon juice, and ⅛ teaspoon of salt.

In a food processor, combine the flours, shortening, coconut sugar, cinnamon, and remaining ¼ teaspoon of salt. Pulse until the mixture begins to come together like a crumbly dough. Add the sliced tigernuts and pulse a few times, just until it looks like there's oatmeal in it.

Scrape the rhubarb mixture into an ungreased 10-inch (26 cm) quiche pan, or a regular 8 × 8-inch (20 × 20 cm) glass pan. Spread the crumble mixture evenly over the top.

Bake, uncovered, for 45 minutes. Let cool completely to set before serving. Refrigerate leftovers. The topping will solidify more under refrigeration.

SPICED PEACH CRUMBLE

This delicious crumble is made with warm spices and frozen peaches—so it can be made any time of year. It will hold together better chilled, but if you like it warm, top it with some AIP ice cream. So, so yummy.

- 4 cups (1 pound, or 454 g) frozen peach slices
- ½ cup (120 ml) water
- 1 tablespoon (15 ml) fresh lemon juice
- 1 tablespoon (15 ml) honey
- ¾ teaspoon sea salt, divided
- 1½ teaspoons ground cinnamon, divided
- ½ teaspoon ground ginger
- ¼ teaspoon ground cloves
- 2 teaspoons (6 g) arrowroot flour
- ½ cup (50 g) tigernut flour
- ⅓ cup (43 g) cassava flour
- ⅓ cup (68 g) organic palm shortening
- ¼ cup (36 g) coconut sugar
- ¼ cup (24 g) sliced tigernuts

Preheat the oven to 350°F (175°C or gas mark 4).

In a large saucepan over medium heat, combine the frozen peaches, water, lemon juice, honey, ½ teaspoon of salt, 1 teaspoon of cinnamon, the ginger, and cloves. Heat for 7 minutes, stirring.

Make a well in the center of the peach mixture and whisk in the arrowroot, ensuring there are no lumps. Stir to combine. Spread the fruit mixture evenly in the bottom of an ungreased 8 × 8-inch (20 × 20 cm) glass pan.

In a food processor, combine the flours, shortening, coconut sugar, sliced tigernuts, remaining ¼ teaspoon of salt, and remaining ½ teaspoon of cinnamon. Process until everything is combined and crumbly. Spread this mixture evenly over the fruit mixture.

Bake for 30 minutes. Let cool completely to set before serving.

. . . .

CHAPTER 9

QUICK BREADS

. . . .

I must tell you the truth: AIP breads can be challenging. You already knew that, though, didn't you? I discovered that one reason breads are so difficult in AIP baking is their sheer size. Without gluten and eggs, breads can still easily rise, but lack the structure necessary to hold their shape. Cutting down their size by making mini loaves solves this, and it helps you keep your sugar intake reasonable. Think small!

With that little disclaimer out of the way, BREADS! If there's one recipe you should try from this chapter, it's got to be the Bagels (page 146). They're a little bit of a project, but you'll have bagels for breakfast, sandwich holders for lunch, and burger buns for dinner! Note that when they are first done, they will seem way too soft, maybe even gummy. Give them some time in the fridge and *voilà!* Bread!

BAGELS

This is not a drill, my bread-craving friends. These are real bagels! Before AIP, I made bagels frequently, and oh how I've missed them. But now, we can alllllll make bagels! They are easy, but they will require of you one thing: patience. You will want to dig in as soon as they come out of the oven, but the weird thing is that they work better the next day, unlike traditional breads. That's AIP baking. Upside-down and backward!

3   **tablespoons (27 g) coconut sugar, divided**

1   **cup (152 g) cassava flour**

½   **cup (59 g) arrowroot flour**

¼   **cup (24 g) tigernut flour**

1   **teaspoon rapid-rise yeast**

½   **teaspoon sea salt**

½   **teaspoon cream of tartar**

1   **cup (240 ml) hot (not boiling) water**

Preheat the oven to 400°F (200°C or gas mark 6). Line a roasting sheet with parchment paper.

Place 1 tablespoon (9 g) of coconut sugar in a large pot of water (about 4 quarts, or 3.8 L) over high heat. Tip: Covering the pot as it heats will bring it to a boil faster.

In a food processor, combine the remaining 2 tablespoons (18 g) of coconut sugar and the rest of the dry ingredients. Pulse a few times to incorporate. With the food processor running, slowly add the hot water through the feeder tube. Continue to process until about 30 seconds after the dough has formed. Turn off the processor, *but leave it closed.* Let sit for 5 minutes.

Turn the dough onto a clean work surface. You should not need any flour on your surface. Divide the dough into 4 equal portions and roll each it into a ball. Flatten slightly to 1½ inches (3.5 cm).

With the bagel shape on the work surface, stick a finger through the middle, holding the dough with your other hand. Twirl your finger a bit to increase the center hole size to ¾ inch (2 cm).

Your water should be boiling. Carefully place the bagels, two at a time, in the boiling water. They will sink at first. Use a utensil to keep them from sticking to the bottom. When the bagels rise fully to the surface of the water, start a timer for 1 minute. Gently flip them over at the 30-second mark. Scoop the bagels out of the water with a slotted spoon or a spider. Place them on the roasting sheet.

Bake for 15 minutes, turn them over, and bake for 15 minutes more.

Let cool completely before you even *think* about cutting into them. After the bagels have cooled, place them in a zip-top bag. After several hours, or overnight, they will be firm enough to cut with a serrated knife.

BANANA BREAD

Any kind of bread on the autoimmune protocol is a bit of a unicorn—a mythical creature. It took me many, many tries to get this recipe to work. Tip: To reduce cracking on the top of this bread, smooth the batter with moistened fingers before putting it into the oven.

¾ cup (97 g) cassava flour

¾ cup (87 g) tigernut flour

¾ cup (75 g) coconut flour

1½ teaspoons grass-fed gelatin

1½ teaspoons baking soda

½ teaspoon sea salt

½ teaspoon cream of tartar

1½ cups (338 g) mashed ripe banana

¼ cup (60 ml) extra-virgin olive oil

¼ cup (60 ml) pure maple syrup

1 tablespoon (15 ml) apple cider vinegar

Preheat the oven to 350°F (175°C or gas mark 4). Line an 8½ × 4½-inch (21 × 11 cm) glass loaf pan with parchment paper.

In a large bowl, combine the flours, gelatin, baking soda, salt, and cream of tartar. Stir in the banana, oil, syrup, and vinegar. Spread the batter evenly into the prepared loaf pan. The batter will be thick.

Bake, uncovered, for 30 minutes. Tent the pan loosely with aluminum foil. Bake for 20 minutes, or until a toothpick inserted into the center comes out clean. Let the bread cool completely in the pan before removing it and cutting to serve.

CAULIFLOWER PIZZA CRUST

Think of this crust as your canvas. You can put anything on it, not just the traditional pizza toppings. You might add herbs to the crust. You might also use it, cut up, as a vessel for sliders, or a sandwich. Brush it with some olive oil, add your toppings, then pop it under the broiler for a few minutes to your desired doneness. It is very filling, so one crust will be plenty for one person. Make one for now and freeze one for later.

1 tablespoon (9 g) coconut sugar

2 tablespoons (30 ml) very warm water

1½ teaspoons rapid-rise yeast

1½ cups (198 g) fresh, riced cauliflower (see note)

1 cup (152 g) cassava flour

½ cup plus 1 tablespoon (60 g) coconut flour

½ cup (60 g) tapioca flour

6 tablespoons (90 ml) extra-virgin olive oil

6 tablespoons (90 ml) room temperature water

1 teaspoon sea salt

Preheat the oven to 450°F (230°C or gas mark 8). Line a large baking sheet with parchment paper.

In a small bowl, dissolve the coconut sugar in the warm water. Stir in the yeast and let sit for 5 minutes. If the yeast does not foam up, throw it away and start over. Your water could be too hot or cold, or the yeast may be old.

In a food processor, combine the remaining ingredients. Add the yeast mixture. Process until a dough forms, stopping to scrape down the bowl, as needed.

Turn the dough out onto a piece of parchment paper. Gather the dough in your hands and divide it in half. Working with one half of the dough at a time, roll the dough between 2 pieces of parchment paper to 8 inches (20 cm) in diameter. Place the rolled dough on the prepared baking sheet. Repeat with the second half of dough. There should be just enough room for both crusts on the baking sheet.

Bake for 15 minutes. Let cool on the sheet.

+ I use riced cauliflower available in the produce section of the grocery store. If you prefer to make your own, place the cauliflower in a food processor and pulse until it is the consistency of rice.

ZUCCHINI BREAD

Years ago, my family made a zucchini bread recipe that was handed down from my great-aunt, who lived on a farm in Wisconsin. The bread was laden with oil and sugar, but oh so good. This recipe is as close as I can come to that family recipe without going overboard—and being AIP friendly, too!

Organic palm shortening for greasing (optional)

½ cup (54 g) tigernut flour

½ cup (58 g) tapioca flour

⅓ cup (50 g) coconut sugar

¼ cup (26 g) coconut flour

1 tablespoon (10 g) grass-fed gelatin

1½ teaspoons ground cinnamon

½ teaspoon baking soda

¼ teaspoon sea salt

¼ teaspoon cream of tartar

½ cup (60 g) grated zucchini

¼ cup (60 ml) extra-virgin olive oil

¼ cup (60 ml) water

1 tablespoon (15 ml) apple cider vinegar

1 teaspoon organic vanilla extract

Preheat the oven to 350°F (175°C or gas mark 4). Grease a 5¾ × 3-inch (15 × 7.5 cm) mini loaf pan with shortening, or line it with parchment paper.

In a large bowl, whisk the tigernut flour, tapioca flour, coconut sugar, coconut flour, gelatin, cinnamon, baking soda, salt, and cream of tartar to blend, ensuring there are no lumps. Stir in the zucchini, oil, water, vinegar, and vanilla. The batter will be thick. Spread the batter evenly in the prepared loaf pan.

Bake for 20 minutes. Tent the pan loosely with aluminum foil. Bake for 25 minutes, or until a toothpick inserted into the center of the loaf comes out clean; a few tiny crumbs are okay.

Let the bread cool completely in the pan before removing it and serving.

RECIPE IMAGE APPEARS ON PAGE 27.

BANANA "CHOCOLATE" SWIRL BREAD

If you can't decide between plain banana bread or a chocolatey one, swirl them together! I'd be lying if I told you this recipe is easy. Repeat after me: "Perfection is not the aim." Have some fun with it! Just don't swirl too much, or the batters will blend together. Tip: To reduce cracking on the top of this bread, smooth the batter with moistened fingers before putting it into the oven.

1 cup (133 g) cassava flour

¾ cup (87 g) tigernut flour

½ cup (50 g) coconut flour

1½ teaspoons grass-fed gelatin

1½ teaspoons baking soda

½ teaspoon sea salt

½ teaspoon cream of tartar

1½ cups (338 g) mashed ripe banana

¼ cup (60 ml) extra-virgin olive oil

4 tablespoons (60 ml) pure maple syrup, divided

1 tablespoon (15 ml) apple cider vinegar

1 tablespoon (4 g) carob powder or cocoa powder (if successfully reintroduced)

Preheat the oven to 350°F (175°C or gas mark 4). Line an 8½ × 4½-inch (21 × 11 cm) glass loaf pan with parchment paper.

In a large bowl, combine the flours, gelatin, baking soda, salt, and cream of tartar. Thoroughly stir in the banana, oil, 3 tablespoons (45 ml) of syrup, and the vinegar. The batter will be quite thick—almost a dough.

Scoop out 1 cup (248 g) of batter and place it in a small bowl. Stir in the remaining 1 tablespoon (15 ml) of syrup and the carob powder.

Spread the plain batter evenly in the prepared loaf pan. Place dollops of carob batter onto the plain batter. Using a table knife, slice through and turn over the batter, lengthwise and crosswise, two or three times to create a swirl effect. Don't swirl too much, or it will be a muddy mess! Smooth the top.

Bake for 30 minutes, uncovered. Tent the pan loosely with aluminum foil. Bake for 20 minutes more, or until a toothpick inserted into the center comes out clean. Let the bread cool completely in the pan before removing it and cutting to serve.

CRANBERRY ORANGE SPICE BREAD

Remember how we talked about keeping baked goods small? This sweet, fragrant bread is an excellent example of how going smaller can be helpful. We'll use a small nonstick loaf pan for this recipe. This loaf is perfect for a holiday brunch.

Organic palm shortening for greasing

- 1 cup (103 g) tigernut flour
- ½ cup (58 g) tapioca flour
- 1 teaspoon ground cinnamon
- ½ teaspoon baking soda
- ¼ teaspoon sea salt
- ¼ teaspoon cream of tartar
- ⅛ teaspoon ground cloves

Grated zest of 1 orange

- 6 tablespoons (90 ml) water, divided
- 1 tablespoon (10 g) grass-fed gelatin
- ¼ cup (36 g) coconut sugar
- 2 tablespoons (30 ml) fresh orange juice
- ½ teaspoon (2 ml) organic vanilla extract
- ¼ cup (60 ml) extra-virgin olive oil
- ¼ cup (32 g) dried cranberries (no added oils or sugars), chopped

Preheat the oven to 350°F (175°C or gas mark 4). Grease a 5¾ × 3-inch (15 × 7.5 cm) nonstick loaf pan.

In a large bowl, whisk the flours, cinnamon, baking soda, salt, cream of tartar, cloves, and orange zest to blend.

Pour 2 tablespoons (30 ml) of water into a cold saucepan. Sprinkle in the gelatin and let sit for 2 minutes to "bloom." Place the saucepan over medium-low heat. Cook, gently whisking, until all the gelatin has liquified. Immediately transfer to a stand mixer fitted with a whisk attachment and whisk at high speed for 30 seconds. With the mixer running, gradually add the coconut sugar, orange juice, and vanilla. Pour in the oil in a small stream and mix until incorporated.

Turn the mixer to low speed. Little by little, add the dry ingredients, stopping to scrape down the bowl, as needed. Gradually add the remaining 4 tablespoons (60 ml) of water. Turn the mixer to medium-high speed and mix until the batter is an even consistency.

Turn off the mixer and remove the bowl. Stir in the cranberries. Scrape the batter into the prepared loaf pan and spread it evenly.

Bake for 20 minutes. Tent the pan loosely with aluminum foil. Bake for 15 to 20 minutes, or until a toothpick inserted into the center of the bread comes out clean. Let the bread cool in the pan before removing it. Let cool completely before slicing to serve.

. . . .

CHAPTER 10

CRACKERS & SNACKS

. . . .

When we're traveling or going from one activity to the next, it can be tempting to chuck the healing diet out the car window and grab something that may set us back. Having AIP crackers and snacks around can be so useful, especially while on the go. These recipes are easy to put together, and very nice to grab when you are feeling snacky. You'll find many different styles here, from traditional Graham Crackers (page 163) to "Cheese" Straws (page 159) to the unique Lavender Thyme Rounds (page 164). Satisfy your need to nosh here. In moderation, of course.

CASSAVA LAVOSH CRACKERS

These crackers are very easy to make, and totally addictive. I even have to keep my non-AIP family away from them. I dare you not to eat them all at once!

½ cup plus 1 tablespoon (79 g) cassava flour, plus more as needed

½ teaspoon sea salt, plus more for sprinkling

½ teaspoon dried basil

½ teaspoon dried oregano

¼ teaspoon onion powder

¼ teaspoon garlic powder

2½ tablespoons (37 ml) extra-virgin olive oil, divided

6 tablespoons (90 ml) warm water

Preheat the oven to 350°F (175°C or gas mark 4). Line a roasting tray with a silicone mat or parchment paper.

In a large bowl, whisk the flour, salt, basil, oregano, onion powder, and garlic powder to blend. Pour in 2 tablespoons (30 ml) of oil and the water. Mix with a fork. You should have a workable dough. Note: The dough should not be sticky. If it is, add more flour, 1 tablespoon (9 g) at a time.

Divide the dough in half and make 2 patties. One at a time, roll the patties between 2 pieces of parchment paper to ⅛ inch (3 mm) thick—no thicker! Don't worry if they crack a bit.

Place the dough sheets on the prepared tray. Brush with the remaining ½ tablespoon (7 ml) of oil and sprinkle with salt.

Bake for 25 minutes, or until golden brown and breakable. Let cool, then break into pieces. Store in an airtight container.

"CHEESE" STRAWS

These beauties are fun to serve when you have guests who are gluten- and dairy-free. These straws are lovely on a charcuterie board, either arranged flat or served upright in a jar. Of course, you can always treat yourself like you treat your guests and make a beautiful plate for a mindful snack.

½ cup (67 g) cassava flour

¼ cup (20 g) large-flake nutritional yeast

½ teaspoon sea salt

½ teaspoon dried basil

½ teaspoon garlic powder

¼ teaspoon ground turmeric

¼ cup (60 ml) water

3 tablespoons (45 ml) extra-virgin olive oil

Preheat the oven to 350°F (175°C or gas mark 4).

In a large bowl, whisk the cassava flour, nutritional yeast, salt, basil, garlic powder, and turmeric to blend. Pour in the water and oil. Mix thoroughly with a fork.

Using your hands, form the dough into a ball. Place the dough on a piece of parchment paper and shape it into a rectangle. Place another piece of parchment on top of the dough. Roll the dough until it is about 5 × 7 inches (13 × 18 cm), and just a little thinner than ¼ inch (6 mm). Remove the top piece of parchment and place it on a baking sheet.

From the long edge of the dough, cut ½-inch (1 cm) strip. It should be roughly ½ × 5 inches (1 × 12.5 cm). Carefully twist it twice, place it on the parchment-lined baking sheet, and gently press the ends onto the paper. Repeat, cutting ½-inch (1 cm) strips, twisting, and pressing.

Bake for 20 minutes. Let cool before serving. Store in an airtight container.

"CHEESY" PUFFS

These cute little guys are savory, and they play well as an appetizer, served next to briny things such as olives or homemade pickles. For a little extra zhuzh factor, sprinkle with a few Maldon sea salt flakes before baking.

½ cup (67 g) cassava flour

¼ cup (20 g) large-flake nutritional yeast

2 tablespoons (18 g) arrow-root flour

½ teaspoon sea salt

¼ cup (60 ml) warm water

3 tablespoons (45 ml) extra-virgin olive oil

Maldon sea salt flakes for garnish (optional)

Preheat the oven to 350°F (175°C or gas mark 4).

In a large bowl, combine the cassava flour, nutritional yeast, arrowroot, and salt. Pour in the water and oil and mix thoroughly with a fork.

Using a 1¼-inch (3 cm) cookie scoop, portion the dough, roll firmly into balls, and place them on an ungreased baking sheet. Sprinkle a few flakes of Maldon sea salt (if using) on each puff.

Bake for 17 minutes. Let cool completely before serving. Store in an airtight container.

GINGER TURMERIC CRACKERS

Caution! Strong flavors here. These snacks, kind of a cross between a cracker and a cookie, are spicy due to the ginger. The flavors pair well with Asian dishes, and would be happy next to some tea, ginger beef soup, or AIP ramen.

½ cup (67 g) cassava flour

1 teaspoon ground ginger

½ teaspoon sea salt

¼ teaspoon ground turmeric

2 tablespoons (30 ml) warm water

2 tablespoons (30 ml) extra-virgin olive oil

2 tablespoons (30 ml) honey

Kelp granules for garnish (optional)

Preheat the oven to 325°F (165°C or gas mark 3). Line a baking sheet with parchment paper.

In a large bowl, combine the flour, ginger, salt, and turmeric. Pour in the water, oil, and honey and mix with a fork.

Using a 1¼-inch (3 cm) cookie scoop, portion the dough onto the prepared baking sheet. Press each portion to ¼ inch (6 mm) thick using three fingers.

Sprinkle each very lightly with kelp granules (if using).

Bake for 20 minutes. Let cool before serving. Store in an airtight container.

GRAHAM CRACKERS

Yay! Graham crackers! Try them with sliced banana and some tigernut spread, such as the one from Tigernut Butter and Jam Sammies (page 80).

- ½ **cup plus 1 tablespoon (83 g) cassava flour**
- ½ **cup (58 g) tigernut flour**
- ½ **cup (72 g) coconut sugar**
- ¼ **cup (60 ml) extra-virgin olive oil**
- ¼ **cup (60 ml) water**
- 2 **teaspoons (6 g) grass-fed gelatin**
- ½ **teaspoon baking soda**
- ¼ **teaspoon ground cinnamon**
- ¼ **teaspoon organic vanilla extract**

Preheat the oven to 325°F (165°C or gas mark 3).

In a food processor, combine the flours, coconut sugar, oil, water, gelatin, baking soda, cinnamon, and vanilla. Pulse a couple of times, then turn the processor on until the ingredients are smooth and form a barely sticky dough. Stop to scrape down the bowl, as needed.

Roll the dough between 2 pieces of parchment paper to ⅛ inch (3 mm)—no thicker! If it is thicker, the crackers will taste fine, but they won't get crispy.

Remove the top layer of parchment. Find the center point of the dough. Using a pizza wheel or a fluted pastry wheel, make a cut up the center of the rolled dough. Measure 2 inches (5 cm) from the center and make another cut. Measure another 2 inches (5 cm) and make another cut. Repeat on the other side.

Turn the parchment and repeat the cutting process, making cuts at 2 inches (5 cm). You should now have 16 square crackers, plus some ragged edges. Don't remove those. We'll need them.

With a toothpick, create 5 holes in each cracker, in the pattern similar to dice. Slide the entire piece of parchment, with the dough on it, onto a baking sheet.

Bake for 25 minutes. Let the crackers cool completely. Break off the ragged edges, which have likely browned. Carefully break apart the crackers. Store in an airtight container.

RECIPE IMAGE APPEARS ON PAGE 17.

LAVENDER THYME ROUNDS

These light and crispy crackers are lovely with tea or by themselves. Lavender can be a strong flavor, so I've kept the amount small, and offset it with thyme—kind of Provençal!

½ cup (67 g) cassava flour, plus more as needed

1 teaspoon organic food-grade dried lavender

1 teaspoon dried thyme

½ teaspoon sea salt

¼ teaspoon onion powder

¼ cup (60 ml) water

2 tablespoons (30 ml) extra-virgin olive oil

Preheat the oven to 325°F (165°C or gas mark 3).

In a large bowl, whisk the flour, lavender, thyme, salt, and onion powder to blend. Pour in the water and oil and mix thoroughly with a fork. You should have a workable dough that is not sticky. If needed, add more flour.

Place a sheet of parchment paper on a work surface. Using a tablespoon measure, scoop the dough onto the parchment, leaving space between each. Place a second piece of parchment on top. Using the bottom of a glass or a measuring cup, flatten each ball to ⅛ inch (3 mm) thick and 2½ inches (6 cm) in diameter. Gently lift off the top piece of parchment. Slide the bottom piece with the rounds onto a baking sheet.

Bake for 25 minutes, or until the rounds are crisp. Let cool. Store in an airtight container.

RECIPE IMAGE APPEARS ON PAGE 13.

LEMON TARRAGON CRACKERS

These crackers are surprisingly zesty. The lemon and tarragon notes go well with fish. Try them topped with smoked mussels or some seafood spread.

½ cup (67 g) cassava flour, plus more as needed

1 teaspoon dried tarragon
  Grated zest of 1 lemon

½ teaspoon sea salt

¼ teaspoon baking soda

⅛ teaspoon garlic powder

2 tablespoons (30 ml) water

2 tablespoons (30 ml) fresh lemon juice

2 tablespoons (30 ml) extra-virgin olive oil

Preheat the oven to 350°F (175°C or gas mark 4).

In a large bowl, whisk the cassava flour, tarragon, lemon zest, salt, baking soda, and garlic powder to blend. Pour in the water, lemon juice, and oil and mix thoroughly with a fork. The dough should be workable and not sticky. If it is, add more flour.

Roll the dough between 2 sheets of parchment to ⅛ inch (3 mm) thick. Lift off the top piece of parchment and place it on a baking sheet. Using a 2-inch (5 cm) round or fluted cookie cutter, cut out shapes, and carefully place them on the parchment-lined baking sheet. Pierce the center of each cracker one time with a fork.

Bake for 20 minutes, or until crisp. Let cool. Store in an airtight container.

PESTO PINWHEELS

A lovely accompaniment to soup or as an appetizer, these pesto pinwheels are punchy and flavorful. These are best served freshly made.

1 cup (40 g) loosely packed fresh basil leaves

3 garlic cloves, roughly chopped

4 tablespoons (60 ml) extra-virgin olive oil, divided

½ teaspoon large-flake nutritional yeast

⅛ teaspoon sea salt, plus ½ teaspoon

½ cup (67 g) cassava flour, plus more as needed

¼ cup (60 ml) warm water

Preheat the oven to 350°F (175°C or gas mark 4).

In a mini food processor, combine the basil, garlic, 2 tablespoons (30 ml) of oil, nutritional yeast, and ⅛ teaspoon of salt. Whirl until almost a paste, stopping to scrape down the bowl, as needed.

In a large bowl, combine the cassava flour and remaining ½ teaspoon of salt. Pour in the remaining 2 tablespoons (20 ml) of oil and the water. Mix thoroughly with a fork. The dough should not be sticky. If it is, add a bit more flour.

Place a piece of parchment paper on a work surface and place the dough on it. Form the dough into a square with your hands. Place another piece of parchment on top of the dough. Roll the dough into a 6 × 6-inch (15 × 15 cm) square. Tip: The dough will want to roll into a circle, so you may need to push it with a straight edge back into a square shape and roll it again.

When you've got the right shape, remove the top layer of parchment and place it on a baking sheet. The bottom layer of parchment remains as a work surface. Spread the pesto mixture over the dough, leaving a ½-inch border along one edge only.

Starting with the side opposite the border and ending with bare dough, carefully roll up the dough. If the dough cracks while rolling it, that's normal. Once you have a rolled log, cut it horizontally into ½-inch (1 cm) slices.

To cut, tuck a length of baker's twine or unflavored and unwaxed dental floss under the log ½ inch (1 cm) from the end. Cross the ends over the top of the roll only once. Pull each end outward to make slices. Using the twine method rather than a knife will keep your pinwheels round rather than squished and flat. Place the 12 pinwheels on the parchment-lined baking sheet.

Bake for 20 minutes. Let cool before serving.

ROSEMARY OLIVE OIL CRACKERS

I hesitate to call these crackers. They are almost a savory cookie! If you want to top them, try liver pâté or some olive tapenade.

- ½ cup (67 g) cassava flour, plus more as needed
- 2 teaspoons (1 g) finely chopped fresh rosemary leaves
- ½ teaspoon sea salt
- ¼ teaspoon onion powder
- ¼ teaspoon garlic powder
- 3 tablespoons (45 ml) water
- 3 tablespoons (45 ml) extra-virgin olive oil

Preheat the oven to 325°F (165°C or gas mark 3). Line a baking sheet with parchment paper.

In a large bowl, whisk the cassava flour, rosemary, salt, onion powder, and garlic powder to blend. Pour in the water and oil and mix thoroughly with a fork. The dough should not be sticky. If it is, add more flour.

Roll the dough into a rope 9 inches (23 cm) long and 1 inch (2.5 cm) in diameter. Cut the rope into 12 pieces and place them on the prepared baking sheet. Make crosshatch marks on each piece with a fork, as you would a peanut butter cookie, pressing them to ¼ inch (6 mm) tall.

Bake for 25 minutes, or until mostly crisp. Let cool. Store in an airtight container. The crackers will harden after a couple of days; these are best served fresh.

PLANTAIN PUFFS

These crunchy little snacks are customizable. Once you've made the dough, you can sprinkle the puffs with whatever you like before baking: smoked salt, vanilla salt, plain salt, even nutritional yeast for a cheesy flavor.

2 cups (182 g) bagged plantain chips

½ cup (67 g) cassava flour

½ teaspoon sea salt

¼ teaspoon onion powder

¼ teaspoon garlic powder

6 tablespoons (90 ml) water

2 tablespoons (30 ml) extra-virgin olive oil

Smoked salt, vanilla salt, plain sea salt, or nutritional yeast for sprinkling (optional)

Preheat the oven to 350°F (175°C or gas mark 4).

Place the plantain chips in a food processor. Pulse until the chips are crumbled to the size of corn flakes. Alternatively, crush the chips in a plastic bag with a rolling pin or meat tenderizer.

In a large bowl, combine the flour, salt, onion powder, and garlic powder. Stir in the crushed chips, water, and oil. Scoop the dough by the teaspoonful and roll it into 1-inch (2.5 cm) balls. Place them on an ungreased baking sheet. Sprinkle with flavoring (if using).

Bake for 30 minutes. Let cool before serving. Store in an airtight container.

ABOUT THE AUTHOR

Wendi Washington-Hunt is an AIP foodie, food photographer, author, and recipe developer. When Hashimoto's thyroiditis entered her life, she began diet and lifestyle changes to help her condition. Now, Wendi lives happily in an empty nest in North Carolina with one amazing husband and one spoiled yellow lab, where she spends her time making food and taking pictures of it.

Before becoming a food photographer and a blogger at Wendi's AIP Kitchen, Wendi was a professional opera singer, martial arts practitioner, and piano and voice teacher. She has used these experiences to inspire her creativity and to encourage others to make a mess in their kitchens. It is her passion to help readers savor this new way of eating, rather than being restricted by it.

ACKNOWLEDGMENTS

This book is in existence largely because I have the most supportive husband in the world. Thank you, dearest, for encouraging me when I had recipe flops, tasting all the AIP things when you'd rather have some glutenous sourdough, and offering me your honest feedback, which I have come to trust implicitly over the years. Thank you for supporting this and other dreams. Thank you for sticking with me, and peeling me off the floor when certain recipes failed *again*, and I didn't yet know how to fix them. You are My Favorite. Always.

Thank you to my daughters for cheering me on, and not being too mad that the baked goods in our house were replaced with AIP baking. You are the reason I smile every day. Thank you for making me a mom. There will always be hugs here for you, and chocolate chip cookies.

Thank you, Mom and Dad, for always being the wind in my sails, blowing me in the direction of my dreams. Steph and Greg, thank you for the random phone calls to see how I'm doing, for being subjected to too many food photos, and for being the best cheer squad a sister could have.

Thank you to Dr. Sarah Ballantyne and the pioneers of the AIP movement, who showed me a better way to live with autoimmune disease. I am well aware that I am standing on your shoulders. Thank you for forging the path.

Thank you to Erik Gilg, Jill Alexander, Heather Godin, and the rest of the amazing team at Fair Winds. Thank you for taking a chance on this newbie author, patiently answering a million questions, and bringing this dream to life.

INDEX